ASS TRAVEL GUIDE 2025

Discover Assisi's Accommodations, tourist attractions and spots. Practical Tips and Local Insights

Julienne Lemelin

All rights reserved. No part of this book may be reproduced, stored in a retrieval system, or transmitted in any form or by any means, electronic, mechanical, photocopying, recording, or otherwise, without the prior written permission of the copyright owner. The information contained in this book is for general information purposes only. The author and publisher make no representations or warranties of any kind, express or implied, about the completeness, accuracy, reliability, suitability or availability with respect to the book or the information, products, services, or related graphics contained in the book for any purpose. Any reliance you place on such information is therefore strictly at your own risk.

Copyright © 2025 by Julienne Lemelin

Table of Contents

Introduction 5
   History & Customs 5
Chapter 1: Planning Your Trip 9
   Time to visit 9
   Visa and Entry Requirements 12
   What to pack 16
   Discovering Assisi's Neighborhoods: Where to Stay for an Unforgettable Experience 20
   Hotels in Assisi 24
   Hostels in Assisi: A Traveler's Haven for Comfort and Community 35
Chapter 2: Top Tourist Attractions & Spots in Assisi 45
Chapter 3: Gastronomic Delight & Entertainment 58
   Local Dishes to Try Out in Assisi 58
   Local Drinks to Try Out in Assisi: A Flavorful Sip of Umbria 63
   Discovering Culinary Delights in Assisi 67
   Exploring Street Food in Assisi: A Delightful Journey for Food Lovers 75
   Food Markets in Assisi 85
   Bars and Pubs in Assisi 90
   Nightclubs in Assisi 99
Chapter 4: Travel Itineraries 109

Outdoor Adventure Itinerary in Assisi: A Personal Journey 109

A Romantic Itinerary in Assisi 113

Coastal Itinerary in Assisi: A Journey Through Charm and Serenity 118

Budget-friendly itinerary in Assisi 123

Historical Itinerary in Assisi 127

A Family-Friendly Itinerary in Assisi: A Journey of Wonder and Togetherness 131

Chapter 5: Cultural Experiences 136

Festivals in Assisi: A Journey Through Tradition, Celebration, and Spirit 136

Museums and Galleries in Assisi 141

Off-the-Beaten-Path Attractions in Assisi 151

Chapter 6: Practical Information 162

Safety and Security Considerations 162

Money Matters and Currency Exchange 166

Transportation & Getting Around in Assisi 169

Health Precautions 175

Emergency contact numbers 178

INTRODUCTION

History & Customs

Nestled in the heart of Italy, Assisi is a place where time seems to stand still, its cobbled streets whispering tales of the past. The first time I visited, I was immediately struck by the town's serene atmosphere. It's not just the history that captivates you, though Assisi has that in abundance; it's the spirit of the place, something that lingers in the air and leaves a lasting impression. Walking through the streets, I felt a profound sense of connection—not only to the people who live there today but also to those who shaped its history centuries ago.

Assisi is, of course, synonymous with St. Francis, its most famous son. Born Giovanni di Pietro di Bernardone in the late 12th century, St. Francis abandoned a life of privilege to embrace poverty, preaching a message of humility and care for all living things. As you explore the Basilica of St. Francis, you can't help but be moved. The frescoes by Giotto and Cimabue are breathtaking, telling stories that seem to leap off the walls. I remember standing in the lower basilica, feeling dwarfed by the artistry and the reverence of the place. It's not just a church; it's a shrine to compassion and humanity.

The history of Assisi stretches back far beyond St. Francis, though. Its roots lie in ancient Umbrian settlements, long before the Romans arrived. You can see traces of this in the Roman Temple of Minerva, which still stands proudly in the Piazza del Comune. The first time I saw it, I marveled at how seamlessly the town's history has woven together. Here was a Roman temple, later transformed into a Christian church, standing alongside medieval buildings—a perfect metaphor for Assisi's layered identity. It's fascinating how the town has preserved its past without feeling like a museum. Life goes on here, bustling and vibrant, even as history peeks out from every corner.

What struck me most, though, was the customs of the people. There's a rhythm to life in Assisi that feels different, slower, and more intentional. Early in the morning, I would see shopkeepers sweeping their stoops, chatting with neighbors as they prepared for the day. It felt like a scene out of another era, yet completely genuine. The local markets are a treasure trove, where vendors sell everything from fresh produce to handmade crafts. I bought a small ceramic bowl from an elderly woman who told me with pride that her family had been making pottery in Assisi for generations. It's this kind of connection to tradition that gives the town its soul.

Festivals in Assisi are something else entirely—a celebration of history, faith, and community. One of the most memorable experiences I had was during the Calendimaggio festival, which takes place every May. The whole town transforms into a medieval wonderland, with parades, music, and reenactments that transport you back in time. People dress in elaborate costumes, their enthusiasm infectious. I joined a group of locals for a traditional dance in the square, laughing as I stumbled over the steps. It was such a joyful moment, a reminder that history isn't just something we study—it's something we live.

The people of Assisi are deeply connected to their faith, and it permeates every aspect of life here. The first time I attended a Mass in the Basilica of St. Clare, I was moved to tears, even though I couldn't understand every word. The nuns' singing was otherworldly, their voices echoing through the ancient stone walls. St. Clare, a follower of St. Francis, founded the Poor Clares, a contemplative order that continues to thrive in Assisi. Her story, one of courage and devotion, is as inspiring as that of St. Francis himself.

But Assisi isn't just about grand churches and saints. It's in the small things, too—the way the sun sets over the Umbrian hills, bathing the town in golden light; the sound of footsteps on ancient stone; the smell of freshly baked bread wafting from a tiny bakery. I spent an afternoon wandering aimlessly, discovering hidden courtyards and quiet corners. At one point, I stumbled upon a small vineyard, where an old man was pruning vines. We exchanged smiles, and he offered me a handful of grapes. They were the sweetest I'd ever tasted, and for a moment, it felt like I'd stepped into a painting.

The food in Assisi deserves a mention, too. Meals here are a celebration, not just of flavors but of togetherness. I remember sitting down to dinner at a small trattoria, the kind of place where the menu is handwritten and the wine comes from a nearby vineyard. The owner, a cheerful woman named Maria, insisted I try the strangozzi al tartufo, a local pasta dish with black truffle. It was simple yet exquisite, every bite a testament to the region's culinary heritage. Sharing stories with fellow diners, I realized that food in Assisi is more than sustenance—it's a bridge that connects people.

One evening, I joined a local family for a meal, an experience I'll never forget. They welcomed me like an old friend, despite the language barrier. We ate, drank, and laughed late into the night, their warmth making me feel like I belonged. They told me stories about their ancestors, about life in Assisi during World War II, about how the town has changed and stayed the same. It was in those moments that I understood the true heart of Assisi—its people.

Assisi is also a place of pilgrimage, and you see this in the steady stream of visitors from around the world. But it never feels overcrowded or touristy. There's a sense of respect here, a quiet understanding that this is a place of significance. Even as I explored the bustling Piazza del Comune or hiked up to the Rocca Maggiore, a medieval fortress with stunning views of the valley, I felt a sense of peace. It's as if Assisi has its own rhythm, one that gently pulls you in and invites you to slow down.

I spent my last morning in Assisi walking along the town's ancient walls, taking in the panoramic views of the Umbrian countryside. It was early, and the mist still hung low over the fields, giving everything a dreamlike quality. I thought about all the history this town has witnessed, all the lives that have been lived here. It's humbling, in a way, to stand in a place that has endured for so long, to feel like a small part of its story.

As I left Assisi, I carried with me more than just memories. I carried the lessons of its history, the warmth of its people, and the beauty of its customs. It's a place that leaves a mark on your soul, a reminder of what truly matters. Whether you're drawn by faith, history, or simply the desire to experience something extraordinary, Assisi has a way of making you feel at home, even if just for a little while. And isn't that the magic of travel—to find pieces of yourself in places you've never been?

CHAPTER 1: PLANNING YOUR TRIP

Time to visit

Assisi, a picturesque hill town in the heart of Italy's Umbria region, is a place that captures the imagination the moment you arrive. Choosing the best time to visit depends on what you want to experience, but each season offers its own magic. Having spent time wandering its cobblestone streets, soaking in the charm of this spiritual haven, I can tell you there's no wrong time to visit—but each season paints Assisi in a different light.

The first time I visited Assisi, it was early spring, and I remember the gentle hum of the countryside awakening from its winter slumber. The hills were dotted with wildflowers, and the air carried the faintest scent of blossoming trees. It wasn't too cold, nor was it particularly warm—just the kind of crisp weather that makes a light jacket and scarf your best companions. Walking up to the Basilica of St. Francis, the soft light of the morning sun made the honey-colored stone glow in a way that felt almost sacred. The crowds were still manageable in March, allowing me to linger in front of frescoes by Giotto without feeling rushed. There's something about seeing those centuries-old masterpieces in relative quiet that makes you appreciate their power even more.

As spring progressed into April and May, Assisi grew busier, but it never felt overwhelming. This time of year is ideal for anyone who loves gardens and nature. The olive groves and vineyards surrounding the town begin to burst into vibrant green, and the countryside feels alive. I took a hike along the trails leading up Monte Subasio, the mountain that cradles Assisi, and was rewarded with breathtaking views of the town below. The birdsong and the rustle of leaves in the breeze made it feel as though I had stepped into a pastoral painting.

Summer in Assisi has its own rhythm. When I visited in June, the heat was starting to build, but the early mornings and evenings remained cool and inviting. This is the season of long, sun-drenched days, and the town feels festive and alive. Tour groups flock to the main sites like the Basilica of Santa Chiara and the Piazza del Comune, but if you know how to time your day, you can still find moments of peace. I made it a habit to explore in the early morning, before the day's heat fully arrived. Strolling through the narrow alleys with their flower-filled balconies was a quiet, meditative experience.

By mid-afternoon, when the sun was at its peak, I sought refuge in Assisi's quieter corners. There's a small café near the Rocca Maggiore fortress where I spent hours sipping iced coffee and gazing out at the rolling hills of Umbria. The fortress itself offers panoramic views that make the climb worthwhile, especially if you time it for sunset. Watching the sun dip below the horizon, casting the landscape in hues of gold and pink, is a memory that still feels vivid in my mind.

August, though hot, is when Assisi becomes a hub of activity. Ferragosto, the traditional Italian holiday season, brings an influx of visitors, but it's also when the town hosts its vibrant festivals. I happened to be there during a reenactment of medieval life, complete with processions and traditional costumes. The streets came alive with music, laughter, and the scent of local delicacies being prepared. It felt as though I had stepped back in time, and the sense of community and celebration was infectious.

When September arrived, I found Assisi in a gentler mood. The summer crowds thinned, and the temperature became more forgiving. This is harvest season, and the surrounding countryside buzzed with activity as farmers prepared to pick grapes and olives. I joined a small tour to visit a family-run vineyard, where I tasted wines that carried the very essence of the Umbrian soil. Autumn in Assisi is for food lovers; the markets brim with fresh produce, truffles, and chestnuts. Every meal felt like a celebration of the season.

October, with its cooler weather, brought a different kind of beauty. The trees began to turn golden, and the town felt quieter, more reflective. This is a wonderful time for spiritual seekers or anyone looking to experience Assisi at a slower pace. Walking the Via San Francesco, the path connecting key religious sites, felt especially poignant in the autumn light. The Pilgrim's Trail, as it's often called, took me through serene landscapes that seemed tailor-made for introspection.

Winter in Assisi, I discovered, is a season of contrasts. The mornings were often misty, lending a mystical quality to the town's ancient stone walls. By afternoon, the sun would break through, casting long shadows and creating a dramatic play of light and dark. The Basilica of St. Francis, which had felt bustling during the warmer months, was now almost eerily quiet. I found myself lingering in its lower crypt, where the tomb of St. Francis is located, and felt a deep sense of peace.

December is particularly special because of the holiday season. The nativity scenes, or presepi, displayed around the town range from traditional to highly artistic. One evening, I stumbled upon a live nativity scene being enacted in the Piazza San Rufino. The flickering torchlight and the sound of carols made it a magical moment, one that felt uniquely tied to the spirit of Assisi.

January and February are the coldest months, and while the chill can be biting, the town feels wonderfully authentic. This is when Assisi belongs to its residents, and as a visitor, you get a glimpse of everyday life. I found it the perfect time to explore the town's lesser-known churches, like San Damiano, where St. Francis first heard his calling. The quiet allowed me to reflect, and I left feeling a deeper connection to the history and spirituality of the place.

Each visit to Assisi has left me with a different impression, shaped by the season. Whether it was the awakening of spring, the vibrant energy of summer, the golden embrace of autumn, or the quiet intimacy of winter, Assisi revealed a new facet of itself each time. The town has a way of drawing you in, of making you slow down and appreciate the beauty in the details—the play of light on a stone wall, the taste of freshly baked bread, the echo of footsteps in an empty piazza.

If I were to choose one time of year to visit, it would depend entirely on what you're seeking. For a lively atmosphere, late spring and summer are ideal. If you prefer a quieter, more contemplative experience, the cooler months of autumn and winter hold a special charm. But no matter when you go, Assisi has a way of leaving an indelible mark on your heart, just as it has on mine. It's a place where time seems to stand still, where the past and present coexist in perfect harmony, and where every season tells its own story.

Visa and Entry Requirements

Assisi is one of those enchanting destinations that draws you in with its charm, history, and serene atmosphere. When planning a trip to this remarkable Italian town, nestled in the heart of Umbria, one of the first things to sort out is the visa and entry requirements. While this might sound like a mundane detail compared to the thought of walking in the footsteps of St. Francis or exploring centuries-old architecture, trust me—it's a crucial step that can make or break your dream of visiting Assisi.

Let me start by saying that navigating the visa process for Italy, and consequently for Assisi, isn't as intimidating as it might seem at first glance. I've been there, scrolling through pages of embassy websites, trying to make sense of the requirements, and worrying about whether I've ticked all the right boxes. But once you understand the process and know what to expect, it becomes a straightforward part of your travel preparation.

The first thing to consider is your nationality and where you're traveling from. If you're from a country within the European Union or the Schengen Area, the good news is that you won't need a visa to enter Italy. You can just pack your bags and go, using your passport or national ID card to get through immigration. It feels incredibly liberating knowing you can simply show up and start exploring Assisi's cobbled streets and breathtaking basilicas without any added bureaucracy.

For travelers from outside the EU or Schengen Area, like myself, the situation is a little different. I needed to apply for a Schengen Visa because Italy is part of this zone, which allows you to travel to multiple countries in Europe with just one visa. This might seem overwhelming initially, but it's actually a huge convenience if you're planning to explore more than just Assisi during your trip. I remember meticulously putting together my application—a process that required careful attention to detail but was ultimately very manageable.

The first step for me was to figure out where to apply. Since I was planning to spend the majority of my time in Italy, including several days in Assisi, I needed to apply for my Schengen Visa through the Italian consulate or visa center in my home country. It's essential to apply through the country where you'll spend the most time or where your journey begins, so double-check your itinerary before submitting your application.

The application form itself is pretty standard. It asks for basic details like your name, passport number, travel dates, and purpose of the visit. I filled it out online and printed it, ensuring I double-checked every entry to avoid errors. When it comes to supporting documents, this is where being organized makes all the difference.

You'll need to provide a valid passport with at least two blank pages and validity extending three months beyond your intended stay. I also had to submit proof of travel insurance—something that's non-negotiable for Schengen visas. The policy needs to cover a minimum of €30,000 in medical expenses, including emergencies and repatriation. It might sound excessive, but having this kind of coverage is reassuring, especially when traveling to a place like Assisi where you'll want to enjoy every moment without worrying about unexpected mishaps.

Another essential requirement was proof of accommodation. I booked a charming guesthouse in Assisi's old town and included the reservation confirmation with my application. Even if you're planning to stay in multiple places, make sure you have a booking confirmation for each one. The visa officers want to see that you have a clear plan and won't end up stranded somewhere. I also had to provide proof of financial means, which meant submitting recent bank statements and a letter from my employer to show I had a stable income and enough funds for the trip. It might feel invasive, but these documents help prove you're visiting as a genuine tourist and not overstaying your welcome.

One thing that surprised me was the importance of an itinerary. Even though Assisi was my primary destination, I included a detailed outline of my plans, listing not just the sights I wanted to visit but also transportation details and any day trips I was considering. For example, I mentioned my intention to visit the Basilica of St. Francis, walk through the ancient streets, and explore nearby towns like Spello and Perugia. This showed that I had a purpose for my trip and that I'd planned it thoroughly.

Once I had all my documents ready, I booked an appointment to submit them in person. This is where the process can feel a bit nerve-wracking, especially if you're not used to dealing with consulates or visa centers. But the staff were surprisingly helpful and guided me through the submission process. After submitting my application, I had to provide biometric data—fingerprints and a photograph. It's a standard part of the process and only took a few minutes.

Waiting for the visa to be processed was perhaps the most anxious part of the journey. It took about two weeks to hear back, which felt like an eternity when you're excited about your trip. I kept checking my email and tracking my application status online, hoping for good news. When the visa was finally approved, the relief and excitement were indescribable. Holding that little sticker in my passport made all the effort worthwhile.

When I finally arrived in Italy, the entry process was smooth. At the immigration counter, the officer took a quick look at my visa, scanned my passport, and asked a few basic questions about the purpose of my visit. I told them I was heading to Assisi to soak in its spiritual and historical ambiance, and that was it—I was on my way.

Looking back, I realize how important it was to start the visa process early. Depending on your nationality, the requirements and processing times can vary, so it's always better to allow plenty of time to gather your documents and schedule your appointment. For me, starting about two months before my travel date gave me enough time to handle unexpected delays or additional document requests.

One final tip I'd share is to always carry copies of your visa and supporting documents with you during your trip. Although I didn't face any issues while in Assisi, it's better to have them on hand just in case. You never know when a hotel might ask for proof of your visa or if you'll need it for some unforeseen reason.

In the end, the effort to navigate the visa process was well worth it. Stepping into Assisi felt like stepping into a different time—a place where history, art, and spirituality converge. Whether you're marveling at the frescoes in the Basilica of St. Francis, wandering through quiet alleys, or taking in the panoramic views of the Umbrian countryside, you'll find that all the paperwork and preparation fade into the background. What stays with you is the magic of Assisi and the profound sense of peace it offers. If anything, the visa process becomes just another part of the story, one that adds to the anticipation and excitement of finally experiencing this extraordinary destination.

What to pack

Packing for a trip to Assisi is an experience unto itself. Imagine stepping into the heart of Italy's Umbria region, where time slows down and every cobblestone feels like it has a story to tell. If you're like me, preparing for a visit to a place as historic and picturesque as Assisi isn't just about throwing random items into a bag—it's about envisioning yourself wandering through its ancient streets, breathing in the crisp countryside air, and soaking in the peacefulness that seems to radiate from every corner.

When I packed for my first trip to Assisi, I thought a lot about the balance between practicality and immersion. This isn't just any destination; it's a place where the charm of medieval architecture meets the spirituality of centuries-old basilicas. You'll walk a lot in Assisi. Trust me, those winding streets and breathtaking viewpoints will call to you, and you'll want to explore every nook and cranny. Comfortable shoes became my best friend. I packed a pair of sturdy sneakers for the uneven terrain and cobblestones, along with a more lightweight pair for strolling in the evenings when the streets feel quieter, almost like they belong to you alone.

Layering was another game-changer. The weather in Assisi can shift dramatically depending on the season, and even within a single day, you might feel like you've experienced all four seasons.

I visited in the spring, and I remember how chilly the mornings were as the mist clung to the hills. By midday, the sun warmed everything up, and I was grateful for a light jacket that could be easily slipped off and carried around. A scarf became my secret weapon—not just for keeping warm when the wind picked up but also as a way to cover my shoulders when entering churches like the Basilica of St. Francis, where modest attire is a sign of respect.

Speaking of respect, I packed clothes that felt both comfortable and appropriate. Assisi has a timeless elegance to it, and you'll notice that the locals carry themselves with a quiet sophistication. I stuck to casual but polished outfits—think breathable fabrics like linen or cotton in neutral tones that didn't scream "tourist." A good pair of trousers or a long skirt came in handy for blending in, especially when enjoying a leisurely meal at a trattoria overlooking the valley. If you're planning to spend time outdoors, perhaps hiking up to Rocca Maggiore for panoramic views of the countryside, consider packing activewear or at least something you don't mind getting a bit dusty.

Now, let's talk about the practical items that made my trip smoother. A small daypack became my go-to for carrying essentials during the day—water, a guidebook, some snacks, and, of course, my camera. Assisi is unbelievably photogenic, and I found myself constantly reaching for my camera to capture the golden light spilling over terracotta rooftops or the intricate frescoes inside the basilicas. If you're a photography enthusiast like me, don't forget spare batteries or a portable charger. There's nothing worse than your camera dying just as the perfect shot presents itself.

I also brought a reusable water bottle, which turned out to be a brilliant decision. Assisi has several fountains with fresh drinking water, and there's something incredibly satisfying about refilling your bottle from a centuries-old stone fountain. It made me feel like I was truly living in the moment, partaking in a simple ritual that locals have been doing for generations.

One thing I wish I'd thought of earlier was a small notebook. Assisi has this way of stirring something in you, whether it's the quiet beauty of the Basilica of Santa Chiara or the serenity of the olive groves that stretch out towards the horizon. I found myself jotting down impressions, little snippets of thoughts that I wanted to hold on to. A journal became not just a keepsake but also a way to deepen my connection with the place.

For those who, like me, can't resist sampling local delicacies, packing a few reusable food containers or zip-lock bags might sound strange, but hear me out. Assisi's markets are brimming with fresh produce, cheeses, and pastries, and it's all too easy to pick up more than you can eat in one sitting. I still remember the delight of unwrapping a wedge of pecorino cheese later in the day, accompanied by a crisp apple from the market. It's those little moments that stay with you long after you've left.

Electronics were another thing I thought carefully about. While my phone was indispensable for maps and quick photos, I made it a point to disconnect as much as possible. Assisi invites a slower pace of life, and I wanted to honor that. A simple watch helped me keep track of time without constantly pulling out my phone, and a universal adapter ensured that my devices stayed charged. If you're planning to use your phone extensively, a local SIM card or an international plan can save you from hefty roaming fees.

Toiletries are always a personal choice, but I'd recommend keeping things minimal. I stuck to the essentials—travel-sized versions of my favorite products—and packed them in a clear, reusable pouch to make airport security a breeze. Sunscreen was non-negotiable, even in the cooler months, as the Italian sun can be deceptively strong. A small tube of hand cream was another lifesaver; walking around all day left my hands feeling dry, and a little self-care goes a long way.

One thing I didn't fully anticipate was how much I'd appreciate having a small stash of snacks with me. Assisi is full of charming cafés and trattorias, but sometimes you find yourself in a quiet corner of the town, away from the main squares, and hunger strikes. A handful of nuts or a granola bar tucked into my daypack came to the rescue more than once. If you have dietary restrictions, this is especially important—though I must say, Italy is wonderfully accommodating when it comes to food.

And then there are the small, often-overlooked items that ended up being surprisingly useful. A compact umbrella, for instance, came in handy when an unexpected shower swept through the town. A lightweight tote bag proved invaluable for carrying souvenirs—like the delicate ceramic tiles and handwoven textiles that Assisi is famous for. I also carried a travel-size laundry kit, just in case I needed to freshen up my clothes mid-trip. It might sound unnecessary, but when you're traveling light, being able to wash and re-wear your favorite outfit is a game-changer.

Finally, I'd say don't forget to pack your sense of curiosity and openness. Assisi has a way of revealing itself slowly, layer by layer. It's not just the grand basilicas or the sweeping views that will capture your heart, but the small, quiet moments—the echo of your footsteps in a medieval alley, the warm smile of a shopkeeper, the scent of freshly baked bread wafting from a family-run bakery. Packing thoughtfully allows you to embrace those moments fully, without the distractions of discomfort or unpreparedness.

Looking back, packing for Assisi felt less like a chore and more like a prelude to the adventure that awaited me. It was an exercise in mindfulness, in considering not just what I would need but also how I wanted to experience this remarkable place. So, as you prepare for your journey, take a moment to picture yourself there—walking those storied streets, savoring every detail—and let that vision guide you. It's a trip that will stay with you forever, and starting it with the right essentials will make all the difference.

Discovering Assisi's Neighborhoods: Where to Stay for an Unforgettable Experience

When planning a visit to Assisi, the first thing to consider is where to stay to make the most of this charming Umbrian town. Assisi isn't a sprawling metropolis; instead, it's a beautifully compact gem perched on a hill, with neighborhoods that offer distinct vibes and experiences. After exploring its cobblestone streets, rolling countryside, and spiritual heart, I can confidently share my insights on the best areas to stay. Whether you're looking for history, tranquility, or a bustling hub, there's a corner of Assisi perfect for you.

1. Centro Storico (Historic Center)

If you want to stay in the heart of Assisi, there's no better place than the **Centro Storico**. This is where history whispers through every stone, and stepping out of your accommodation feels like entering a medieval dream. Walking through the narrow alleys, you'll find beautifully preserved architecture, quaint shops, and cozy cafes.

I stayed here on my first trip to Assisi, in a charming guesthouse just steps away from the Basilica of Saint Francis. Waking up to the sound of church bells was magical. Everything is within walking distance – from the Piazza del Comune, the bustling square with its Roman Temple of Minerva, to artisan boutiques selling handmade ceramics. The streets are alive during the day but fall silent and serene in the evening, giving you a sense of stepping back in time.

Why Stay Here?

- **Best For:** History lovers, spiritual seekers, and those wanting to immerse themselves in Assisi's charm.
- **What to Expect:** Narrow streets, limited car access, and steep walks – bring comfortable shoes!
- **Insider Tip:** Look for accommodations with rooftop terraces; the views over the Umbrian valley are breathtaking, especially at sunset.

2. Santa Maria degli Angeli

A few kilometers downhill from Assisi's historic center lies the neighborhood of **Santa Maria degli Angeli**. This area is home to the grand Basilica of Santa Maria degli Angeli, which houses the Porziuncola – the tiny chapel where Saint Francis started his spiritual journey.

This neighborhood feels more modern compared to the Centro Storico, with wider streets, better parking options, and larger hotels. I stayed here during a festival, and the proximity to the train station made it incredibly convenient. It's quieter than the bustling hilltop, but still buzzing with life, especially around the basilica.

Why Stay Here?

- **Best For:** Families, travelers with cars, and those seeking convenience.
- **What to Expect:** A mix of modern amenities and spiritual history, with easy access to Assisi and nearby towns.

- **Insider Tip:** Don't miss the evening mass at the basilica – it's a moving experience even if you're not religious.

3. San Damiano and the Olive Groves

For those who crave peace and a deeper connection to nature, consider staying near **San Damiano**, on the outskirts of Assisi. This area is quieter, surrounded by olive groves and rolling hills, and feels worlds away from the busy town center.

During one of my visits, I stayed in a countryside agriturismo here, and it was soul-soothing. Imagine waking up to the sound of birds, sipping your morning coffee while overlooking olive trees, and strolling down peaceful paths to the church of San Damiano, where Saint Francis is said to have received his divine calling.

Why Stay Here?

- **Best For:** Nature lovers, writers, and anyone seeking solitude.
- **What to Expect:** Rustic charm, a slower pace, and limited public transport – it's best to have a car.
- **Insider Tip:** Pack a picnic and enjoy it in the olive groves; it's an unforgettable experience.

4. Piazza Santa Chiara Area

Near the Basilica of Saint Clare (Santa Chiara), this neighborhood offers a quieter alternative to the bustling Piazza del Comune. Staying here means you're close to the church dedicated to Saint Clare, the founder of the Poor Clares, and her tomb.

I stayed in a family-run bed-and-breakfast here, and the hospitality was unmatched. The views from Piazza Santa Chiara, stretching across the valley, are some of the best in Assisi. The neighborhood feels less touristy, with more locals going about their daily lives, making it a great place to feel part of the community.

Why Stay Here?

- **Best For:** Couples and solo travelers looking for a serene yet central location.
- **What to Expect:** Intimate accommodations and stunning views over the countryside.
- **Insider Tip:** Try to time your visit with the golden hour – the piazza glows beautifully in the evening light.

5. Eremo delle Carceri (Hermitage Retreat)

If you're the adventurous type or seeking a truly off-the-beaten-path experience, consider staying near the **Eremo delle Carceri**. Located on Mount Subasio, this hermitage is where Saint Francis and his followers would retreat for prayer and contemplation. While accommodations are sparse, there are a few eco-friendly lodges and retreats in the area.

I spent a day hiking up here and envied those staying overnight, surrounded by lush forests and complete tranquility. The silence is profound, broken only by the rustling of leaves or the occasional bird song.

Why Stay Here?

- **Best For:** Hikers, spiritual retreats, and eco-conscious travelers.
- **What to Expect:** Remote settings, rustic lodgings, and a connection to nature.
- **Insider Tip:** Bring a good pair of hiking boots and a journal – it's a place that inspires reflection.

6. Spello – A Neighboring Gem

While not technically part of Assisi, the nearby town of **Spello** is a fantastic alternative for those seeking a quieter base. Just a short drive or train ride away, Spello offers similar medieval charm but with fewer crowds.

On one visit, I stayed in Spello and commuted to Assisi daily. The town is famous for its flower festival, **Infiorate**, where the streets are decorated with intricate floral designs. Staying here allowed me to enjoy Assisi's highlights while retreating to a peaceful, picturesque village at the end of the day.

Why Stay Here?

- **Best For:** Travelers seeking tranquility with easy access to Assisi.
- **What to Expect:** Quiet streets, local dining, and stunning views of the Umbrian valley.
- **Insider Tip:** Visit the local wine bars – Spello is known for its excellent wines.

Hotels in Assisi

Visiting Assisi, a town drenched in history, spirituality, and charm, is a dream come true. From the breathtaking Basilica of St. Francis to the cobblestone streets lined with ancient buildings, this Italian gem offers experiences like no other. But where to stay? Well, during my time there, I explored several delightful hotels, each with its own personality and offerings. Whether you're seeking luxury, history, or budget-friendly charm, there's something for everyone. Let me walk you through some of the hotels I either stayed at or visited during my trip.

Hotel: Nun Assisi Relais & Spa Museum

- **Address:** Via Eremo delle Carceri, 1A, 06081 Assisi PG, Italy
- **Contact:** +39 075 8155150
- **Website:** www.nunassisi.com
- **Average Nightly Rate:** €250–€400
- **Amenities:** Luxury spa, indoor pool, fitness center, fine dining, complimentary breakfast
- **Star Rating:** ★ ★ ★ ★ ★
- **Check-In/Out Times:** Check-in: 3 PM | Check-out: 11 AM

Let me start with a gem that feels like stepping into a luxurious time machine. Nun Assisi Relais is not just a hotel; it's a historical journey. Built on the ruins of an ancient Roman amphitheater, this boutique hotel blends modern luxury with centuries-old charm. The highlight? The subterranean spa that feels like a secret, tranquil oasis. I spent hours unwinding in their heated pool surrounded by ancient stone walls—an unforgettable experience.

The rooms are equally impressive, combining minimalist elegance with historic accents. If you're looking for indulgence and don't mind splurging, this is the place. The staff? Warm, welcoming, and ready with excellent dining recommendations in town.

Hotel: Hotel Giotto Assisi

- **Address:** Via Fontebella, 41, 06081 Assisi PG, Italy
- **Contact:** +39 075 812209
- **Website:** www.hotelgiottoassisi.com
- **Average Nightly Rate:** €120–€250
- **Amenities:** Rooftop terrace, spa services, onsite restaurant, free Wi-Fi, parking

- **Star Rating:** ★ ★ ★ ★
- **Check-In/Out Times:** Check-in: 2 PM | Check-out: 10:30 AM

Hotel Giotto is perfect if you want panoramic views of the Umbrian valley—waking up to those vistas felt magical. Located just a short walk from the Basilica of St. Francis, this hotel is all about convenience and comfort. Their rooftop terrace is a must for sunsets over the countryside, accompanied by a glass of local wine.

My favorite part? Their restaurant serves an impressive mix of Umbrian specialties and international dishes. After a long day of exploring, I loved unwinding at the spa for a foot massage—heavenly after climbing Assisi's steep streets!

Hotel: Hotel Ideale

- **Address:** Piazza Matteotti, 1, 06081 Assisi PG, Italy
- **Contact:** +39 075 812976
- **Website:** www.hotelideale.com
- **Average Nightly Rate:** €80–€120
- **Amenities:** Garden terrace, free parking, complimentary breakfast, Wi-Fi
- **Star Rating:** ★ ★ ★
- **Check-In/Out Times:** Check-in: 2 PM | Check-out: 10:30 AM

For those looking for budget-friendly charm without compromising on views, Hotel Ideale is the place to be. It's a small, family-run hotel that feels warm and inviting. I particularly loved their garden terrace—it's a perfect spot to sip your morning espresso while enjoying the rolling hills below.

The rooms are simple yet spotless, and the staff went out of their way to make me feel at home. I was traveling solo at the time, and they offered great tips on off-the-beaten-path spots in Assisi. It's not as luxurious as some of the others, but it makes up for it with charm and hospitality.

Hotel: Fontebella Palace Hotel

- **Address:** Via Fontebella, 25, 06081 Assisi PG, Italy
- **Contact:** +39 075 812883
- **Website:** www.fontebellahotel.com
- **Average Nightly Rate:** €100–€180
- **Amenities:** Traditional restaurant, elegant rooms, private parking, Wi-Fi
- **Star Rating:** ★ ★ ★ ★
- **Check-In/Out Times:** Check-in: 3 PM | Check-out: 11 AM

Staying at Fontebella Palace Hotel felt like stepping into an Italian postcard. The 17th-century building oozes character, with arched ceilings, stone walls, and antique furnishings. What stood out for me was their restaurant, Il Frantoio, which serves incredible local dishes like truffle pasta and Umbrian wines.

The rooms are comfortable and maintain a vintage charm. It's close to all the main attractions, and the views over the valley are picture-perfect. The staff are kind and accommodating, always ensuring guests have everything they need.

Hotel: Hotel Pallotta Assisi

- **Address:** Via San Rufino, 6, 06081 Assisi PG, Italy

- **Contact:** +39 075 816553
- **Website:** www.hotelpallotta.com
- **Average Nightly Rate:** €60–€100
- **Amenities:** Rooftop terrace, complimentary breakfast, free Wi-Fi
- **Star Rating:** ✯ ✯ ✯
- **Check-In/Out Times:** Check-in: 12 PM | Check-out: 10:30 AM

If you're traveling on a tight budget but still want to stay in the heart of Assisi, Hotel Pallotta is a delightful option. I was drawn to this hotel for its authentic Italian vibe—it's a small property, but it feels cozy and intimate.

What I loved most was the rooftop terrace. Sitting there with a cappuccino and gazing over the red rooftops of Assisi made me feel like a local. The rooms are small and simple, but they have everything you need for a comfortable stay. Plus, the owner, Sandro, goes above and beyond to make guests feel welcome.

Hotel: Hotel La Terrazza

- **Address:** Via Fratelli Canonichetti, 06081 Assisi PG, Italy
- **Contact:** +39 075 812368
- **Website:** www.laterrazzahotelassisi.com
- **Average Nightly Rate:** €70–€140
- **Amenities:** Outdoor pool, spa, free parking, onsite restaurant, garden
- **Star Rating:** ✯ ✯ ✯
- **Check-In/Out Times:** Check-in: 2 PM | Check-out: 11 AM

For a tranquil retreat just outside the bustling center of Assisi, Hotel La Terrazza is an excellent choice. Nestled in the countryside, it feels like a peaceful escape. I stayed here during the summer, and their outdoor pool was a lifesaver after a day of sightseeing in the heat.

The rooms are spacious and modern, and the garden area is perfect for evening strolls. Their restaurant serves a great mix of local and Mediterranean dishes, and I'd highly recommend their wood-fired pizza. It's a bit farther from the main attractions, but the serenity more than makes up for it.

Hotel: Hotel Alexander

- **Address:** Piazza Chiesa Nuova, 6, 06081 Assisi PG, Italy
- **Contact:** +39 075 816553
- **Website:** www.hotelalexanderassisi.it
- **Average Nightly Rate:** €90–€150
- **Amenities:** Rooftop terrace, free Wi-Fi, complimentary breakfast
- **Star Rating:** ★ ★ ★
- **Check-In/Out Times:** Check-in: 2 PM | Check-out: 10 AM

Hotel Alexander is a little gem located in the heart of Assisi, steps away from the Piazza del Comune. The location couldn't be better—you're surrounded by restaurants, shops, and historic sites.

I loved the clean, modern rooms, but the real highlight was their rooftop terrace. Watching the sun dip behind the hills of Umbria was magical. It's a small hotel with a personal touch, and the staff are incredibly helpful.

Hotel: Grand Hotel Assisi

- **Address:** Via Giovanni Renzi, 2, 06081 Assisi PG, Italy
- **Contact:** +39 075 81501
- **Website:** www.grandhotelassisi.it
- **Average Nightly Rate:** €110–€250
- **Amenities:** Indoor pool, spa, conference facilities, onsite restaurant, free parking, terrace
- **Star Rating:** ✯ ✯ ✯ ✯
- **Check-In/Out Times:** Check-in: 3 PM | Check-out: 11 AM

Grand Hotel Assisi is perfect if you're seeking both comfort and convenience. Nestled on the slopes of Mount Subasio, it offers spectacular views of the valley below. I was impressed by the serene environment—great for unwinding after a long day of sightseeing.

The rooms are spacious and elegant, with large windows that let in plenty of natural light. Their spa facilities are a fantastic bonus; I tried their sauna and left feeling utterly rejuvenated. The onsite restaurant offers traditional Umbrian dishes, and their homemade tiramisu was a highlight.

Hotel: Hotel Windsor Savoia

- **Address:** Viale Marconi, 1, 06081 Assisi PG, Italy
- **Contact:** +39 075 812206
- **Website:** www.windsorsavoia.it
- **Average Nightly Rate:** €80–€160
- **Amenities:** Panoramic terrace, onsite restaurant, free Wi-Fi, parking
- **Star Rating:** ✯ ✯ ✯

- **Check-In/Out Times:** Check-in: 2 PM | Check-out: 11 AM

A family-run establishment since the 1900s, Hotel Windsor Savoia offers a warm, homely vibe with a touch of history. I stayed here during one of my visits and was charmed by its proximity to the Basilica of St. Francis—it's literally a stone's throw away!

The rooms are cozy with traditional furnishings, and the views from the terrace are incredible. Their restaurant serves hearty, home-style meals. I especially enjoyed the truffle risotto, which paired perfectly with a local red wine.

Hotel: Hotel San Francesco

- **Address:** Via San Francesco, 48, 06081 Assisi PG, Italy
- **Contact:** +39 075 812281
- **Website:** www.hotelsanfrancescoassisi.com
- **Average Nightly Rate:** €100–€200
- **Amenities:** Rooftop terrace, onsite restaurant, free Wi-Fi, complimentary breakfast
- **Star Rating:** ★ ★ ★ ★
- **Check-In/Out Times:** Check-in: 3 PM | Check-out: 11 AM

If you're looking to stay steps away from one of the most iconic landmarks in Assisi, Hotel San Francesco is an excellent choice. Located right across from the Basilica of St. Francis, this hotel offers unparalleled convenience and views of the basilica's façade.

The rooftop terrace was my favorite spot to soak in the sunset while sipping on an Aperol spritz. The rooms are modern and comfortable, and the staff are friendly and knowledgeable about local events and attractions.

Hotel: Hotel Porta Nuova

- **Address:** Viale Umberto I, 21, 06081 Assisi PG, Italy
- **Contact:** +39 075 812405
- **Website:** www.hotelportanuova.it
- **Average Nightly Rate:** €90–€150
- **Amenities:** Free parking, garden, complimentary breakfast, free Wi-Fi
- **Star Rating:** ✭ ✭ ✭
- **Check-In/Out Times:** Check-in: 2 PM | Check-out: 10:30 AM

Hotel Porta Nuova is a charming boutique hotel located near the city gate, making it perfect for exploring both the historical center and the surrounding countryside. During my stay, I appreciated the mix of rustic charm and modern amenities.

The rooms are clean and tastefully decorated, with lovely views of the Umbrian valley. Their breakfast spread was fantastic—don't miss the freshly baked pastries. The hotel's garden is a peaceful spot to relax after a day of walking through Assisi's hilly streets.

Hotel: Le Silve di Armenzano

- **Address:** Loc. Armenzano, 06081 Assisi PG, Italy
- **Contact:** +39 075 8019000
- **Website:** www.lesilve.it
- **Average Nightly Rate:** €150–€300
- **Amenities:** Outdoor pool, spa, horse riding, onsite restaurant, hiking trails
- **Star Rating:** ✭ ✭ ✭ ✭
- **Check-In/Out Times:** Check-in: 2 PM | Check-out: 11 AM

If you're looking for an off-the-grid escape, Le Silve di Armenzano is a must-visit. Nestled in the lush greenery of Mount Subasio, this hotel is a haven for nature lovers. I felt like I'd stepped into a dream as I hiked the surrounding trails and enjoyed the serene atmosphere.

The rooms have a rustic-chic aesthetic, blending wooden beams and stone walls with modern comforts. Their restaurant serves farm-to-table meals, and their wine selection is exceptional. This is the perfect place to unwind and reconnect with nature.

Hotel: Hotel Ròseo Assisi

- **Address:** Via Giovanni Renzi, 06181 Assisi PG, Italy
- **Contact:** +39 075 8151
- **Website:** www.roseoassisi.com
- **Average Nightly Rate:** €100–€200
- **Amenities:** Spa, indoor pool, onsite dining, free parking
- **Star Rating:** ★ ★ ★ ★
- **Check-In/Out Times:** Check-in: 3 PM | Check-out: 10 AM

Hotel Ròseo is ideal for those seeking a relaxing stay with excellent amenities. Located slightly outside the town center, it offers a peaceful retreat with easy access to Assisi's attractions.

The spa and wellness center were the highlights for me. After a day of sightseeing, soaking in the pool and indulging in a massage felt like pure bliss. The rooms are spacious and elegantly decorated, with lovely views of the Umbrian hills.

Hotel: Hotel Il Palazzo

- **Address:** Via San Francesco, 8, 06081 Assisi PG, Italy
- **Contact:** +39 075 812803
- **Website:** www.hotelilpalazzoassisi.com
- **Average Nightly Rate:** €80–€150
- **Amenities:** Garden, rooftop terrace, free Wi-Fi, complimentary breakfast
- **Star Rating:** ✯ ✯ ✯
- **Check-In/Out Times:** Check-in: 3 PM | Check-out: 11 AM

Hotel Il Palazzo is a quaint property located in the heart of Assisi's historic center. It's perfect for travelers who want a central location without breaking the bank. I loved the warm, inviting atmosphere and the helpful staff who made sure I had everything I needed.

The rooms are comfortable with a mix of modern and traditional décor. Their rooftop terrace offers gorgeous views of the town and surrounding countryside—it's a great spot for morning coffee or an evening drink.

Hotel: Hotel Da Angelo

- **Address:** Via San Potente, 6, 06081 Assisi PG, Italy
- **Contact:** +39 075 81359
- **Website:** www.hoteldangeloassisi.com
- **Average Nightly Rate:** €70–€120
- **Amenities:** Outdoor pool, onsite restaurant, free parking, Wi-Fi
- **Star Rating:** ✯ ✯ ✯
- **Check-In/Out Times:** Check-in: 2 PM | Check-out: 11 AM

Hotel Da Angelo is a family-run hotel located just outside Assisi's center, offering a warm and welcoming experience. It's a great choice for travelers who prefer a quieter stay with easy access to town.

I particularly enjoyed the outdoor pool, which was perfect for relaxing on warm afternoons. Their restaurant serves hearty Umbrian dishes—I couldn't get enough of their homemade lasagna. The views of the surrounding countryside are lovely, and the staff are incredibly friendly and attentive.

Hostels in Assisi: A Traveler's Haven for Comfort and Community

If you're planning a visit to the picturesque town of Assisi, nestled in the heart of Umbria, Italy, finding the right place to stay can make your experience all the more magical. Assisi is famed for its serene ambiance, historical charm, and breathtaking landscapes, making it a favorite spot for backpackers and budget-conscious travelers. Luckily, the town offers some fantastic hostel options that balance affordability, comfort, and that all-important local charm.

As someone who loves immersing myself in the local vibe, I found Assisi's hostels to be more than just a bed for the night—they were gateways to new friendships, memorable conversations, and insider tips from fellow travelers and welcoming hosts. Here's a curated list of some of the best hostels in Assisi, along with my personal impressions to help you plan your stay.

Hostel: Ostello della Pace

- **Address:** Via di Valecchie 177, Assisi, 06081, Italy
- **Contact:** +39 075 816767
- **Website:** www.ostellodellapace.it
- **Dormitory Rate:** €20-€25 per night
- **Private Room Rate:** €40-€50 per night
- **Amenities:** Free breakfast, communal kitchen, free Wi-Fi, outdoor terrace, laundry facilities, bike rentals, library.
- **Check-In/Out Times:** Check-in: 3:00 PM / Check-out: 10:00 AM

When I stayed at **Ostello della Pace**, I was struck by how aptly it lived up to its name—"Hostel of Peace." Tucked away from the bustling town center, this place offers a quiet retreat surrounded by nature. The rustic charm of the building, with its stone walls and simple but cozy interiors, made it feel like a home away from home.

I loved starting my mornings here with a complimentary breakfast featuring local pastries and coffee. One evening, I joined a communal dinner organized by the staff, which turned into a lively cultural exchange with travelers from all over the world. The outdoor terrace was my favorite spot; sitting there with a book and a cup of tea as the sun set over the rolling Umbrian hills felt like pure magic.

Pro tip: The hostel rents bikes, which are perfect for exploring the surrounding countryside or riding into town.

Hostel: Assisi Garden Hostel

- **Address:** Viale Giovanna di Savoia, 8, Assisi, 06081, Italy
- **Contact:** +39 075 812963

- **Website:** www.assisigardenhostel.com
- **Dormitory Rate:** €25-€30 per night
- **Private Room Rate:** €50-€60 per night
- **Amenities:** Garden area, restaurant, free parking, Wi-Fi, lounge area, pet-friendly.
- **Check-In/Out Times:** Check-in: 2:00 PM / Check-out: 10:30 AM

If you've ever dreamed of staying in a place that feels like a hidden garden, **Assisi Garden Hostel** is your answer. It's set in a former monastery, and the building itself is as much a part of Assisi's history as the town's iconic basilica. When I first walked into the property, I was greeted by blooming flowerbeds and a serene garden area, which immediately put me at ease.

The hostel is a bit more upscale compared to traditional backpacker hostels, offering a restaurant that serves mouthwatering Italian cuisine. I still remember their homemade pasta—it was divine! It's also pet-friendly, which was a delightful surprise when I met a fellow traveler's adorable dog in the lounge area.

The location is just a short walk from Assisi's historic center, making it convenient for sightseeing while still offering a peaceful retreat at the end of the day.

Hostel: Cittadella Ospitalità

- **Address:** Via Degli Ancajani, 3, Assisi, 06081, Italy
- **Contact:** +39 075 813231
- **Website:** www.cittadellaospitalita.it
- **Dormitory Rate:** €18-€22 per night
- **Private Room Rate:** €35-€45 per night
- **Amenities:** Free Wi-Fi, library, event spaces, rooftop terrace, cultural workshops, spiritual retreats.

- **Check-In/Out Times:** Check-in: 4:00 PM / Check-out: 10:00 AM

I stayed at **Cittadella Ospitalità** during a quieter leg of my Assisi trip, and it offered an experience like no other. This hostel is part of a larger cultural and spiritual center, so it attracts visitors interested in more than just sightseeing. From workshops on Franciscan history to live music evenings on the rooftop terrace, every day here felt like an opportunity to connect with the town's deeper soul.

The dorms and private rooms are simple but clean, and the library was an unexpected gem where I discovered some rare books on Assisi's history. The highlight for me was the rooftop terrace, which offers sweeping views of Assisi's rooftops and the surrounding countryside—ideal for a contemplative evening.

If you're seeking a balance of affordability and enrichment, this is a fantastic option.

Hostel: La Casa di Francesco

- **Address:** Piazza San Francesco, 3, Assisi, 06081, Italy
- **Contact:** +39 075 812495
- **Website:** www.lacasadifrancesco.it
- **Dormitory Rate:** €20-€25 per night
- **Private Room Rate:** €40-€55 per night
- **Amenities:** Shared kitchen, laundry facilities, lockers, free Wi-Fi, complimentary tea and coffee, family-friendly atmosphere.
- **Check-In/Out Times:** Check-in: 3:00 PM / Check-out: 11:00 AM

La Casa di Francesco sits right at the heart of Assisi, steps away from the Basilica of St. Francis. For a history buff like me, this was an unbeatable location. Staying here felt like being part of the town's living history. Every morning, I'd step out and be greeted by the sight of the basilica bathed in golden light—it doesn't get more magical than that.

The hostel has a warm and welcoming atmosphere, with staff who seem genuinely eager to ensure your stay is memorable. I appreciated the small touches, like complimentary tea and coffee in the communal kitchen and free Wi-Fi that actually worked well (a rarity in some hostels!). The dorms are spacious, with lockers for added security, and the private rooms are great for couples or families.

Hostel: Camere Carli

- **Address:** Via Lorenzo Perosi, 12, Assisi, 06081, Italy
- **Contact:** +39 075 812345
- **Website:** www.camerecarliassisi.com
- **Dormitory Rate:** €22 €28 per night
- **Private Room Rate:** €45-€55 per night
- **Amenities:** Shared lounge, terrace, free Wi-Fi, bike storage, self-catering kitchen, close to hiking trails.
- **Check-In/Out Times:** Check-in: 2:30 PM / Check-out: 10:00 AM

For outdoor enthusiasts like me, **Camere Carli** was a dream. It's located near some of Assisi's most scenic hiking trails, and the hostel itself feels like a cozy mountain lodge. The shared lounge area was where I ended up spending most of my evenings, swapping stories with fellow travelers over a glass of wine.

The hostel's self-catering kitchen came in handy when I wanted to whip up a quick meal after a long hike. They also provide secure bike storage, which is great if you're exploring Assisi's outskirts on two wheels. One of the most memorable aspects of my stay was waking up to birdsong and stepping out onto the terrace to watch the sunrise over the hills—a moment of pure tranquility.

Hostel: Casa Leonori

- **Address:** Via Giosuè Borsi, 11/13, Assisi, 06081, Italy
- **Contact:** +39 075 8043688
- **Website:** www.casaleonori.it
- **Dormitory Rate:** €22-€27 per night
- **Private Room Rate:** €45-€60 per night
- **Amenities:** On-site restaurant, free parking, garden area, air conditioning, conference facilities, free Wi-Fi.
- **Check-In/Out Times:** Check-in: 2:00 PM / Check-out: 10:30 AM

Casa Leonori is a gem I stumbled upon when looking for a quieter, more private experience. This hostel is particularly popular with groups, but as a solo traveler, I found it welcoming and very well-maintained. The rooms are modern and clean, and the garden area provides a peaceful escape after a day of exploring.

The on-site restaurant was a standout for me. Their dinner menu features classic Umbrian dishes prepared with fresh, local ingredients—don't miss their homemade lasagna! If you're traveling by car, the free parking is a huge plus, as Assisi's historic center can be challenging for parking.

This hostel is a bit more "polished" than your typical backpacker accommodation, making it a great choice for those who prefer a touch of elegance while still staying on budget.

Hostel: Camere Toni

- **Address:** Via San Rufino, 13, Assisi, 06081, Italy
- **Contact:** +39 075 812411
- **Website:** www.cameretoniassisi.it
- **Dormitory Rate:** €20-€24 per night
- **Private Room Rate:** €40-€50 per night
- **Amenities:** Free Wi-Fi, terrace, lockers, laundry facilities, shared kitchen, pet-friendly.
- **Check-In/Out Times:** Check-in: 3:00 PM / Check-out: 11:00 AM

Located in the heart of Assisi, **Camere Toni** felt like a cozy Italian guesthouse rather than a typical hostel. The host, Toni, is incredibly friendly and goes out of his way to make everyone feel at home. I loved sitting on the terrace in the evenings with other travelers, sharing stories and enjoying the view of the surrounding hills.

The shared kitchen is fully equipped, which was perfect for preparing budget-friendly meals. For pet owners, this hostel's pet-friendly policy makes it a rare find in Assisi. Whether you're traveling solo, with friends, or even with your furry companion, you'll find this place welcoming and convenient.

Hostel: All'ombra di San Damiano

- **Address:** Via San Damiano, 22, Assisi, 06081, Italy
- **Contact:** +39 075 812833
- **Website:** www.ombredisandamiano.it
- **Dormitory Rate:** €23-€28 per night
- **Private Room Rate:** €45-€55 per night
- **Amenities:** Free breakfast, garden, free Wi-Fi, yoga classes, library, spiritual retreat programs.

- **Check-In/Out Times:** Check-in: 2:00 PM / Check-out: 10:30 AM

When I stayed at **All'ombra di San Damiano**, I quickly realized it's more than just a place to sleep—it's a spiritual retreat in its own right. Located near the serene San Damiano monastery, this hostel offers an environment of tranquility and introspection.

One unique feature is their yoga classes, which take place in the garden area surrounded by olive trees. The complimentary breakfast was simple but satisfying, featuring fresh bread, local jams, and excellent Italian coffee. The library is a quiet haven for those who enjoy reading about Assisi's rich spiritual heritage.

This hostel is perfect if you're looking for a slower pace and an opportunity to connect with Assisi's deeper spiritual essence.

Hostel: La Dimora del Pellegrino

- **Address:** Via Eremo delle Carceri, 21, Assisi, 06081, Italy
- **Contact:** +39 075 813964
- **Website:** www.dimoradelpellegrino.it
- **Dormitory Rate:** €19-€24 per night
- **Private Room Rate:** €40-€50 per night
- **Amenities:** Shared lounge, hiking trail access, communal kitchen, laundry facilities, free parking, free Wi-Fi.
- **Check-In/Out Times:** Check-in: 3:00 PM / Check-out: 10:00 AM

If you're an outdoor enthusiast, **La Dimora del Pellegrino** is the ideal base for exploring Assisi's natural beauty. It's located close to the Eremo delle Carceri (Hermitage of the Prisons), one of my favorite hiking spots in the area.

The hostel itself is cozy and has a communal lounge where travelers gather in the evenings to share stories or plan their next day's adventures. The staff was incredibly helpful, offering maps and tips for nearby hiking trails. I especially appreciated the free parking, as it made accessing the trails much easier.

After a day of exploring, I loved returning to this peaceful retreat to enjoy a meal in their communal kitchen before heading to bed.

Hostel: Locanda di San Francesco

- **Address:** Piazza del Comune, 5, Assisi, 06081, Italy
- **Contact:** +39 075 813295
- **Website:** www.locandadisanfrancesco.it
- **Dormitory Rate:** €25-€30 per night
- **Private Room Rate:** €50-€65 per night
- **Amenities:** Free breakfast, shared kitchen, lockers, free Wi-Fi, lounge area, prime location.
- **Check-In/Out Times:** Check-in: 2:30 PM / Check-out: 11:00 AM

Locanda di San Francesco is all about location, location, location! Situated right on the main square of Piazza del Comune, it puts you in the heart of Assisi's action. I stayed here for two nights and loved how easy it was to explore the town's iconic landmarks on foot.

The dorms are clean and comfortable, and the private rooms are spacious with charming views of the square. The complimentary breakfast, served in their cozy lounge, included fresh croissants and cappuccinos that gave me the perfect start to my day.

This hostel is ideal for travelers who want to be at the center of everything while enjoying modern amenities in a historic setting.

Hostel: Rifugio del Pellegrino

- **Address:** Via Fontebella, 16, Assisi, 06081, Italy
- **Contact:** +39 075 812498
- **Website:** www.rifugioassisi.it
- **Dormitory Rate:** €22-€26 per night
- **Private Room Rate:** €45-€55 per night
- **Amenities:** Free Wi-Fi, garden, shared kitchen, laundry facilities, lockers, pet-friendly.
- **Check-In/Out Times:** Check-in: 3:00 PM / Check-out: 10:00 AM

The **Rifugio del Pellegrino** lives up to its name as a haven for pilgrims. Located near the Basilica di Santa Maria degli Angeli, it offers a mix of convenience and tranquility. I particularly loved their beautiful garden area, where you can relax after a long day of exploring.

The shared kitchen was well-stocked, and I often cooked my meals here while chatting with other travelers. If you're traveling with pets, this hostel's pet-friendly policy is a huge bonus. The staff is friendly and always ready to recommend hidden gems around town.

CHAPTER 2: TOP TOURIST ATTRACTIONS & SPOTS IN ASSISI

Assisi is a mesmerizing hill town in Italy that oozes history, art, and spirituality. Nestled in the heart of Umbria, it is the birthplace of Saint Francis, making it a beacon for pilgrims and history enthusiasts alike. Visiting this charming town is like stepping back in time, with cobblestone streets, medieval architecture, and breathtaking views of the Umbrian valley. Let me take you on a personalized tour of Assisi's top attractions, as if we were exploring this magical town together.

Attraction: Basilica of Saint Francis of Assisi

Address: Piazza Inferiore di San Francesco, 06081 Assisi PG, Italy
Contact: +39 075 819001
Website: www.sanfrancescoassisi.org
Opening Hours: 8:30 AM
Closing Hours: 6:30 PM (seasonal variations apply)
Directions: From the town center, it's about a 10-minute walk. If you're driving, there's parking nearby at Parcheggio Giovanni Paolo II.
Activity Cost: Free entry (donations encouraged)
Additional Info: Guided tours are available for €10. Photography is allowed, but flash is prohibited.

The Basilica of Saint Francis is an absolute must-see. The first time I walked through its imposing Gothic doors, I felt an overwhelming sense of awe. The basilica has two levels: the Upper Church with its breathtaking frescoes by Giotto, and the Lower Church, which exudes a serene spiritual vibe. Don't miss the tomb of Saint Francis below. I recommend visiting early in the morning to avoid crowds and catch the sunlight streaming through the stained glass windows—it's pure magic.

Attraction: Basilica of Santa Chiara

Address: Piazza Santa Chiara, 06081 Assisi PG, Italy
Contact: +39 075 812282
Website: www.assisisantachiara.it
Opening Hours: 7:00 AM
Closing Hours: 7:00 PM
Directions: A short 5-minute walk from Piazza del Comune. Follow the signs pointing towards Santa Chiara.
Activity Cost: Free
Additional Info: The terrace outside offers some of the best panoramic views of the valley below.

Santa Chiara is where Saint Clare, a follower of Saint Francis, rests. Walking into this basilica felt like stepping into a sacred retreat. The pink-and-white-striped façade is a signature feature, but the highlight for me was the crypt where her remains are kept. The original crucifix that spoke to Saint Francis is also displayed here. Before leaving, take a moment to soak in the views from the piazza outside—it's especially stunning at sunset.

Attraction: Piazza del Comune

Address: Piazza del Comune, 06081 Assisi PG, Italy
Opening Hours: Open 24/7
Closing Hours: Open 24/7
Directions: Located in the heart of Assisi, it's easily accessible on foot from most attractions.
Activity Cost: Free

Additional Info: Great spot for people-watching or grabbing a gelato.

The Piazza del Comune is the bustling heartbeat of Assisi. Surrounded by ancient buildings like the Temple of Minerva and the Palazzo dei Priori, it's a lively space where history meets modern-day life. I loved sitting at one of the outdoor cafés, sipping on an espresso while watching locals and tourists mingle. The fountain at the center is a favorite photo spot, and if you're lucky, you might catch a street performance here.

Attraction: Rocca Maggiore

Address: Via della Rocca, 06081 Assisi PG, Italy
Contact: +39 075 815292
Opening Hours: 10:00 AM
Closing Hours: 6:00 PM
Directions: From Piazza del Comune, it's about a 20-minute uphill walk. Wear comfortable shoes, as the path can be steep.
Activity Cost: €6 for adults; €3 for children
Additional Info: Bring water and snacks, as there are no facilities at the top.

For those who love panoramic views and a touch of medieval history, Rocca Maggiore is worth the climb. I remember trekking up the hill on a sunny afternoon, and although it was a bit of a workout, the views from the fortress made it all worthwhile. You can see the entire Umbrian valley spread out like a painting. Inside the fortress, there are winding staircases and ancient rooms to explore. It's like stepping into a medieval adventure.

Attraction: Eremo delle Carceri

Address: Via Eremo delle Carceri, 06081 Assisi PG, Italy
Contact: +39 075 812301
Website: www.eremocarceri.it
Opening Hours: 6:00 AM
Closing Hours: 8:00 PM
Directions: Located about 4 km from the town center, it's a 10-minute drive or a 1-hour walk through beautiful countryside.
Activity Cost: Free (donations welcome)
Additional Info: Wear sturdy shoes if hiking, as the trails can be uneven.

The Eremo delle Carceri is a peaceful hermitage nestled in the woods of Monte Subasio. This was one of my favorite spots in Assisi. Walking along the serene trails where Saint Francis and his followers once meditated, I felt a profound connection to nature and spirituality. The tiny stone chapels and caves are simple yet deeply moving. If you love quiet, reflective spaces, this is a must-visit.

Attraction: Temple of Minerva

Address: Piazza del Comune, 06081 Assisi PG, Italy
Contact: +39 075 813057
Opening Hours: 9:00 AM
Closing Hours: 6:00 PM
Directions: Located within Piazza del Comune, it's easy to spot its grand columns.
Activity Cost: Free
Additional Info: Combine your visit with a stop at nearby shops and cafés.

It's amazing to see how Assisi blends its Roman past with its medieval charm. The Temple of Minerva, with its towering Corinthian columns, is a striking reminder of the town's ancient roots. Stepping inside, you'll find it has been transformed into a Christian church, yet it retains its classical elegance. I spent some time marveling at how history layers itself in this town—where else can you find a Roman temple repurposed for medieval worship?

Attraction: San Damiano

Address: Via San Damiano, 06081 Assisi PG, Italy
Contact: +39 075 812273
Website: www.santuariosandamiano.org
Opening Hours: 7:00 AM
Closing Hours: 7:00 PM
Directions: A 15-minute walk downhill from the town center. Alternatively, you can take a short taxi ride.
Activity Cost: Free (donations encouraged)
Additional Info: Don't miss the gardens—they're incredibly peaceful.

San Damiano is a small, humble church where Saint Francis is said to have received his calling. The simplicity of the place left me in quiet reflection. The original crucifix that inspired Saint Francis is now in Santa Chiara, but this is where it all began. The surrounding gardens are beautifully kept, and it's a tranquil spot to escape the busier parts of town.

Attraction: Pinacoteca Comunale (Municipal Art Gallery)

Address: Piazza del Comune, 06081 Assisi PG, Italy
Contact: +39 075 812534
Opening Hours: 10:00 AM
Closing Hours: 6:00 PM
Directions: Located in Palazzo Vallemani, just off Piazza del Comune.
Activity Cost: €5
Additional Info: Ideal for art lovers; plan for about an hour here.

Art enthusiasts will love the Pinacoteca Comunale. Housed in a historic palace, this gallery features works by local artists and some rare medieval frescoes. I was particularly captivated by the religious art that gives you insight into the cultural and spiritual history of Assisi. It's a quiet, less-crowded attraction, making it perfect for a leisurely visit.

Attraction: Bosco di San Francesco

Address: Via Ponte dei Galli, 06081 Assisi PG, Italy
Contact: +39 075 813157
Website: www.fondoambiente.it
Opening Hours: 10:00 AM
Closing Hours: 7:00 PM
Directions: Adjacent to the Basilica of Saint Francis; follow the signs to the entrance.
Activity Cost: Free (donations accepted)
Additional Info: Bring a picnic—it's a lovely spot to relax.

If you're a nature lover, don't miss the Bosco di San Francesco. This peaceful woodland area is like an outdoor sanctuary. I enjoyed wandering along its shaded paths, listening to birdsong and taking in the sights of ancient stone bridges and small chapels.

The Land Art installation, a spiraling pathway of stones, was a delightful surprise.

Attraction: Basilica of San Rufino

Address: Piazza San Rufino, 3, 06081 Assisi PG, Italy
Contact: +39 075 812283
Website: www.diocesiassisi.it
Opening Hours: 7:00 AM
Closing Hours: 7:00 PM
Directions: A 10-minute walk from Piazza del Comune. The basilica is located at the highest point in town.
Activity Cost: Free
Additional Info: Don't miss the crypt and museum inside for €3.

This lesser-known gem is where Saint Francis and Saint Clare were baptized. The Romanesque architecture of the basilica is striking, but what I loved most was the sense of history as I explored the crypt and saw remnants of ancient Assisi beneath the church. The bell tower offers stunning views of the town if you're willing to climb up!

Attraction: Porziuncola at Santa Maria degli Angeli

Address: Piazza Porziuncola, 1, 06081 Santa Maria degli Angeli PG, Italy
Contact: +39 075 8051430
Website: www.porziuncola.org
Opening Hours: 6:15 AM
Closing Hours: 8:00 PM
Directions: Located about 4 km from Assisi's town center; reachable by bus or a short taxi ride.

Activity Cost: Free
Additional Info: The feast of Saint Francis (October 4th) draws large crowds to this site.

Porziuncola is a small yet incredibly significant chapel housed inside the grand Basilica of Santa Maria degli Angeli. Stepping inside, I was amazed by the contrast between the humble simplicity of the chapel and the grandeur of the basilica enveloping it. This was one of Saint Francis's favorite places, and you can feel his presence here.

Attraction: Chiesa Nuova

Address: Via Sant'Antonio, 1, 06081 Assisi PG, Italy
Contact: +39 075 812283
Opening Hours: 9:00 AM
Closing Hours: 7:00 PM
Directions: Just a 3-minute walk from Piazza del Comune.
Activity Cost: Free
Additional Info: Best visited in the late afternoon when the light highlights the interiors.

Chiesa Nuova, a charming Baroque church, is said to be built on the site of Saint Francis's family home. I found it fascinating to see how his humble beginnings were preserved and revered. The small museum inside displays artifacts related to his life, offering an intimate glimpse into his story.

Attraction: Monte Subasio

Address: Monte Subasio Park, 06081 Assisi PG, Italy
Contact: +39 0743 222727

Website: www.parks.it
Opening Hours: Open 24/7
Closing Hours: Open 24/7
Directions: A short drive or hike from the town center. Many trails begin near Eremo delle Carceri.
Activity Cost: Free
Additional Info: Ideal for hiking, picnicking, or even paragliding for the adventurous.

Monte Subasio is more than just a mountain—it's a natural haven filled with olive groves, wildflowers, and sweeping views of Umbria. I spent an afternoon hiking one of the many trails, feeling like I was walking through the landscapes that inspired Saint Francis himself. It's a perfect spot for nature lovers and a breath of fresh air after exploring the town.

Attraction: Assisi Cathedral Museum and Crypt (Museo Diocesano e Cripta di San Rufino)

Address: Piazza San Rufino, 3, 06081 Assisi PG, Italy
Contact: +39 075 812581
Opening Hours: 9:00 AM
Closing Hours: 6:00 PM
Directions: Inside the Basilica of San Rufino, just a short walk uphill from Piazza del Comune.
Activity Cost: €5
Additional Info: Combine this with your visit to the basilica for a deeper dive into its history.

This museum and crypt surprised me with its treasures, from medieval art to ancient Roman relics. Walking through the crypt, I felt as though I was uncovering layers of history hidden beneath Assisi. If you're a history buff, this is a must-see.

Attraction: San Francesco Woodland Path (Sentiero Bosco di San Francesco)

Address: Via Ponte dei Galli, 06081 Assisi PG, Italy
Contact: +39 075 813157
Website: www.fondoambiente.it
Opening Hours: 10:00 AM
Closing Hours: 7:00 PM
Directions: Start at the Basilica of Saint Francis; the trailhead is well-marked.
Activity Cost: Free (donations encouraged)
Additional Info: Wear comfortable walking shoes; the trail is about 3 km long.

Walking this trail felt like stepping into Saint Francis's world. The lush greenery, stone bridges, and small chapels along the path create a meditative atmosphere. The trail ends at the Church of Santa Croce, a hidden gem surrounded by tranquility.

Attraction: Oratorio dei Pellegrini

Address: Via San Francesco, 13, 06081 Assisi PG, Italy
Contact: +39 075 812221
Opening Hours: 9:00 AM
Closing Hours: 6:00 PM
Directions: Located on Via San Francesco, about halfway between the Basilica of Saint Francis and Piazza del Comune.
Activity Cost: Free
Additional Info: This small chapel is often overlooked but worth a quick visit.

This charming oratory is adorned with stunning frescoes that depict the life of Saint Francis and the pilgrims who came to

Assisi. The peaceful interior feels like a hidden sanctuary amid the bustling streets of the town.

Attraction: Sanctuary of Rivotorto

Address: Via del Santuario, 06081 Rivotorto PG, Italy
Contact: +39 075 8051430
Website: www.assisisantuari.org
Opening Hours: 7:00 AM
Closing Hours: 7:00 PM
Directions: A 10-minute drive or 30-minute walk from Assisi town center.
Activity Cost: Free
Additional Info: Best visited in the morning for a peaceful experience.

The Sanctuary of Rivotorto is built around the Sacro Tugurio, the small hut where Saint Francis and his followers first lived. Walking through this modest space, I could imagine the simplicity and humility that defined their lives. The surrounding gardens are a lovely spot to reflect and unwind.

Attraction: Roman Forum and Archaeological Museum

Address: Piazza del Comune, 06081 Assisi PG, Italy
Contact: +39 075 8138680
Website: www.museodiassisi.it
Opening Hours: 10:00 AM
Closing Hours: 6:00 PM
Directions: Access through a stairway in Piazza del Comune.
Activity Cost: €5

Additional Info: Combine with a visit to the Temple of Minerva for a deeper Roman history experience.

This underground museum offers a fascinating glimpse into Assisi's Roman past. The preserved ruins of the forum, complete with columns and ancient inscriptions, are a stark contrast to the medieval architecture above ground. I was amazed at how well the city preserves its multi-layered history.

Attraction: Teatro Metastasio

Address: Piazza Matteotti, 06081 Assisi PG, Italy
Contact: +39 075 8138680
Opening Hours: Varies depending on performances.
Closing Hours: Varies depending on performances.
Directions: Located near Piazza Matteotti; follow signs from the town center.
Activity Cost: Ticket prices vary by performance (€10–€25).
Additional Info: Check schedules in advance; performances often sell out.

For a cultural treat, the Teatro Metastasio offers concerts, plays, and other performances in an intimate setting. I attended a classical music concert here, and the acoustics combined with the historic ambiance made it a memorable evening.

Attraction: Fountain of the Three Lions

Address: Piazza del Comune, 06081 Assisi PG, Italy
Opening Hours: Open 24/7
Closing Hours: Open 24/7
Directions: Located in the center of Piazza del Comune.

Activity Cost: Free
Additional Info: Perfect for photos, especially in the evening when the square is illuminated.

This charming fountain, adorned with three lions, is a focal point of the bustling Piazza del Comune. I loved sitting nearby with a gelato in hand, soaking in the vibrant atmosphere of the square.

CHAPTER 3: GASTRONOMIC DELIGHT & ENTERTAINMENT

Local Dishes to Try Out in Assisi

Assisi, the charming hilltop town in the heart of Umbria, isn't just a pilgrimage site for spiritual seekers—it's also a paradise for food lovers. As you walk through its cobblestone streets, you'll be greeted by the tantalizing aroma of traditional Umbrian dishes wafting from trattorias and family-run osterias. These culinary delights aren't just meals—they are a celebration of Assisi's rich history, local ingredients, and time-honored recipes passed down through generations.

The Flavors of Umbrian Cuisine

Umbrian cuisine is rustic, earthy, and deeply connected to the land. Think fresh herbs, aged cheeses, truffles, olive oil, and hearty meats. Unlike some Italian regions that lean heavily on pasta or seafood, Umbrian dishes are balanced and diverse, reflecting the region's agricultural bounty and culinary traditions.

I still remember my first meal in Assisi—a simple yet exquisite plate of **Strangozzi al Tartufo Nero**, a dish I can't wait to tell you about. Let's dive into the dishes you simply *must* try when visiting this magical town.

Strangozzi al Tartufo Nero (Pasta with Black Truffles)

If there's one dish that defines the culinary soul of Assisi, it's this one. **Strangozzi**, a hand-rolled pasta similar to tagliatelle but thicker, is the star. Tossed in olive oil and generously coated with freshly shaved **black truffles**, this dish is the epitome of luxury in simplicity.

I tried this at a little trattoria near Piazza del Comune, where the chef grated the truffles at my table. The earthy, aromatic truffle combined with the rich Umbrian olive oil was unforgettable. Pair it with a glass of Sagrantino wine from nearby Montefalco, and you've got yourself a quintessential Assisi experience.

Porchetta

Ah, **porchetta**—a dish so iconic that every bite feels like a celebration. This slow-roasted pork, stuffed with garlic, rosemary, fennel, and other herbs, is juicy on the inside with a perfectly crisp crackling on the outside. Locals often eat it as a filling for sandwiches or serve it sliced with fresh bread.

I discovered the best porchetta stall at a street market in Assisi. The vendor, a cheerful man named Giovanni, handed me a thick slice wrapped in wax paper. The pork was succulent, the herbs vibrant, and the crackling? Oh, the crunch still haunts my dreams.

Zuppa di Lenticchie di Castelluccio (Lentil Soup)

Umbria is famous for its lentils, particularly those from **Castelluccio**, a small village nestled in the Sibillini Mountains. In Assisi, you'll often find these lentils in a hearty soup, flavored with garlic, sage, and a drizzle of olive oil.

One chilly evening, I warmed up with a bowl of this soul-soothing soup at a tiny osteria overlooking the Basilica of St. Francis. The lentils were tender and nutty, and the olive oil added a fruity richness. It's a dish that feels like a hug from Nonna (Italian grandma).

Torta al Testo

Torta al Testo is a traditional Umbrian flatbread, cooked on a **testo**, a flat iron plate heated over an open flame. In Assisi, this bread is often split and stuffed with prosciutto, pecorino cheese, or even grilled vegetables.

I grabbed one from a local bakery and enjoyed it while wandering the streets. The bread was warm, slightly charred, and filled with creamy pecorino and salty ham. It's the perfect on-the-go snack for exploring the town.

Cinghiale in Umido (Stewed Wild Boar)

Umbria is known for its game meat, and **cinghiale** (wild boar) is a regional favorite. Cooked slowly in red wine, tomatoes, and herbs, the result is a rich, tender stew with deep, comforting flavors.

I had my first taste of cinghiale at a family-run restaurant tucked away in a quiet alley. The boar was incredibly tender, with the sauce perfectly balanced between sweet and savory. It was served with a side of **polenta**, which soaked up all that delicious sauce. A culinary memory I'll cherish forever.

Fagiolina del Trasimeno (Lake Trasimeno Beans)

Though humble, the **fagiolina del Trasimeno** is a rare delicacy in Umbria. These small, ivory-colored beans are grown near Lake Trasimeno and are often served as a side dish or in salads.

I encountered these beans in a cold salad paired with cherry tomatoes, basil, and olive oil at a local enoteca. Their slightly nutty flavor and creamy texture made them a surprising highlight of my meal.

Pecorino Cheese

Assisi's rolling hills are dotted with sheep pastures, so it's no wonder that **pecorino cheese** is a staple. You'll find it in many forms—aged, soft, or infused with truffles.

One afternoon, I visited a local cheese shop and sampled slices of pecorino drizzled with honey. The combination of the sharp, salty cheese and the sweet honey was a revelation. Be sure to pick up some to take home; it's a taste of Assisi that will transport you back every time.

Umbrian Olive Oil

Though not a dish, Umbrian olive oil deserves a mention. Its robust, peppery flavor enhances almost every dish in Assisi, from simple bruschetta to rich pastas.

During my visit, I toured an olive grove just outside the town and tasted freshly pressed oil. Dipping warm, crusty bread into that golden-green elixir was a sensory experience like no other. It's no exaggeration to say Umbrian olive oil is liquid gold.

Rocciata

For dessert, **Rocciata** is a must-try. This spiral pastry, filled with apples, nuts, and spices, is often compared to strudel but has a distinct Umbrian touch.

I tried Rocciata at a café near the Basilica of St. Clare. The pastry was flaky, the filling spiced with cinnamon, and the dusting of powdered sugar made it feel festive. It's especially popular during the holidays but can be found year-round.

Tozzetti and Vin Santo

To end your meal, indulge in **tozzetti**—Umbrian almond biscuits—served with a glass of **Vin Santo**, a sweet dessert wine. The custom is to dip the biscuits into the wine, softening them slightly and blending the nutty and sweet flavors.

I discovered this pairing at a small restaurant where the owner explained its significance. "It's not just dessert," she said. "It's a moment to savor life."

Local Drinks to Try Out in Assisi: A Flavorful Sip of Umbria

Assisi isn't just a place to immerse yourself in art, architecture, and spirituality; it's also a fantastic destination to explore authentic Italian flavors, including its delightful local drinks. Wandering through its cobbled streets, you'll notice that every cafe, restaurant, and bar seems to hold the promise of a unique sip that reflects the traditions of Umbria. From luscious wines to refreshing aperitifs and fragrant herbal infusions, Assisi's drink culture feels like a journey all on its own.

Sagrantino Wine: A Must-Try Umbrian Treasure

If there's one drink that represents the very soul of Assisi, it's Sagrantino wine. This bold red wine, made from the Sagrantino grape native to the region, is nothing short of extraordinary. My first encounter with this wine was at a quaint enoteca (wine bar) tucked into the corner of Assisi's historic center. The robust flavor, with notes of blackberry, plum, and a hint of spice, instantly transported me into the rolling vineyards of Montefalco, where the wine originates.

Pro tip: Order a glass of Sagrantino Passito if you prefer a sweeter dessert wine. Its velvety texture and hints of dried fruit are perfect with a slice of Umbrian cheesecake or biscotti.

Prosecco from Umbria: A Sparkling Delight

While Prosecco is traditionally associated with northern Italy, you'll find some delightful local versions in Assisi. During my visit, I discovered a small family-run winery on the outskirts of town offering an Umbrian take on this classic sparkling wine. Sipping a chilled glass of Prosecco on a terrace overlooking the Basilica of St. Francis was an unforgettable moment. The delicate bubbles and crisp apple and pear notes paired beautifully with the view.

Whether you're celebrating a special occasion or simply toasting to the beauty of Assisi, Prosecco is always a good choice.

Limoncello: A Zesty Italian Classic

Though Limoncello hails from southern Italy, Assisi offers its own spin on this vibrant lemon liqueur. I tried a locally crafted version at a tiny trattoria after a hearty meal of truffle pasta, and I must say, it was the perfect digestivo. The liqueur's sweetness balanced the sharp citrus tang, leaving a refreshing finish that lingered pleasantly.

Some places in Assisi even infuse their Limoncello with herbs like rosemary or thyme for a unique twist. If you visit in summer, a frosted glass of chilled Limoncello on a warm evening is pure bliss.

Vin Santo: Sacred Wine for a Sacred City

Assisi is, of course, a city steeped in spirituality, and there's no better way to honor that than by trying Vin Santo, also known as "Holy Wine." Traditionally used in religious ceremonies, this amber-hued dessert wine is made from dried grapes and aged for years to develop its complex, nutty flavor.

I first tasted Vin Santo during an olive oil tasting session at a local agriturismo. Served alongside cantucci (almond biscuits), the pairing was heavenly. The wine's warm, caramelized flavors and slightly viscous texture made it feel like a spiritual experience in itself.

Grappa: A Strong Sip of Tradition

If you're feeling adventurous and ready to embrace a drink with some serious kick, Grappa is the way to go. This distilled spirit, made from grape pomace left over from winemaking, is not for the faint-hearted. I was hesitant at first but decided to give it a try at a rustic osteria recommended by a friendly local.

The bartender served Grappa in a tiny glass, advising me to sip it slowly. It was fiery, yes, but also surprisingly smooth, with floral undertones that complemented the after-dinner ambiance. Grappa is often infused with flavors like honey, herbs, or berries, so if the plain version feels too intense, these variations are worth exploring.

Aperol Spritz: An Aperitivo Classic

Assisi's aperitivo culture is vibrant, and you can't experience it fully without an Aperol Spritz in hand. This bright orange cocktail, a mix of Aperol, Prosecco, and soda water, is a staple in Italian social life. I ordered one at a bustling piazza as the sun set behind the medieval rooftops, and it was the perfect way to wind down after a day of exploring.

Paired with a plate of olives, nuts, and bruschetta, the Aperol Spritz felt like an open invitation to soak in the relaxed rhythms of Italian life. If you're not an Aperol fan, you can opt for a Campari Spritz, which offers a slightly more bitter profile.

Umbrian Craft Beers: A Rising Trend

While Italy is renowned for its wines, Assisi has embraced the growing craft beer movement. Local breweries like Birra Perugia create artisanal beers that reflect the flavors of the region. During a casual dinner at a trattoria, I tried an Umbrian pale ale with hints of citrus and rosemary, and it paired beautifully with my wood-fired pizza.

For beer lovers, a visit to a craft brewery in or around Assisi offers a refreshing change from the usual wine-centric experience.

Herbal Teas and Infusions: A Soothing Alternative

Not all of Assisi's memorable drinks are alcoholic. The city's herbal teas and infusions, often crafted from local ingredients like lavender, sage, and chamomile, are perfect for those seeking a calming experience. I stumbled upon a charming tea house on a rainy afternoon and warmed up with a steaming cup of lavender-infused tea. It was aromatic, soothing, and just what I needed to recharge.

Some cafes even blend their own unique combinations, so don't hesitate to ask for recommendations.

Espresso and Caffè Corretto: The Italian Coffee Ritual

Of course, no discussion of drinks in Assisi would be complete without mentioning espresso. Italians take their coffee seriously, and Assisi is no exception. Morning, noon, or night, you'll find locals savoring tiny cups of rich, aromatic espresso at cafes across town.

For an extra kick, try a caffè corretto, which is espresso "corrected" with a splash of Grappa or Sambuca. I had my first caffè corretto at a tiny cafe near Piazza del Comune, and it was a delightful way to end the day.

Discovering Culinary Delights in Assisi

Assisi, a charming town nestled in the heart of Umbria, is known for its spiritual significance, rich history, and stunning landscapes. But let me tell you, one of the most memorable aspects of my visits has been the food. The restaurants here don't just serve meals; they offer experiences steeped in tradition, creativity, and the warmth of Italian hospitality. Let me take you on a journey through some of my favorite dining spots in Assisi, each with its own unique flavor and charm.

1. Ristorante La Stalla

- **Address**: Via Eremo delle Carceri, 24, Assisi
- **Contact**: +39 075 812317
- **Website**: www.lastallaassisi.it
- **Cuisine Type**: Traditional Umbrian
- **Average Meal Cost**: €25-40
- **Opening Hours**: 12:00 PM – 10:00 PM
- **Reservations**: Recommended, especially for weekends
- **Specialties**: Grilled meats, wild boar stew, truffle pasta

If you're seeking a rustic experience, **Ristorante La Stalla** is a must-visit. Located a short drive from the town center, this restaurant sits amidst lush greenery and exudes countryside charm. On my first visit, the aroma of grilled meats welcomed me before I even stepped through the door. The open grill in the center of the dining area is not just for show – it's where they cook some of the best steaks and sausages I've ever tasted. Don't miss their truffle pasta; it's a perfect harmony of earthy flavors and creamy indulgence.

2. Trattoria Pallotta

- **Address**: Vicolo della Volta Pinta, 3, Assisi
- **Contact**: +39 075 812705
- **Website**: www.trattoriapallotta.com
- **Cuisine Type**: Classic Italian
- **Average Meal Cost**: €20-35
- **Opening Hours**: 12:30 PM – 2:30 PM, 7:30 PM – 10:00 PM
- **Reservations**: Suggested for dinner
- **Specialties**: Strangozzi with black truffle, rabbit stew

Situated in the heart of Assisi, **Trattoria Pallotta** feels like stepping into a warm embrace. The cozy interiors and friendly staff make it an inviting space for a leisurely meal. Their strangozzi, a local pasta, with black truffle is a dish that's hard to forget. The rabbit stew, slow-cooked to perfection, is another highlight. Pair your meal with a glass of local Sagrantino wine – trust me, it's the perfect complement.

3. Osteria Piazzetta dell'Erba

- **Address**: Piazza Matteotti, 3, Assisi
- **Contact**: +39 075 815352
- **Website**: www.piazzettadellerba.it
- **Cuisine Type**: Contemporary Italian
- **Average Meal Cost**: €30-50
- **Opening Hours**: 1:00 PM – 3:00 PM, 7:30 PM – 10:00 PM
- **Reservations**: Necessary during peak season
- **Specialties**: Gourmet tasting menus, homemade ravioli

Osteria Piazzetta dell'Erba is where tradition meets innovation. The chefs here take classic Umbrian recipes and elevate them with modern techniques and presentation. The homemade ravioli stuffed with ricotta and spinach, served with a sage butter sauce, is a work of art. They also offer tasting menus that allow you to explore a variety of flavors in one sitting. Dining here feels like being treated to a masterclass in modern Italian cuisine.

4. Il Baccanale

- **Address**: Piazza San Rufino, 6, Assisi
- **Contact**: +39 075 816600
- **Website**: www.ilbaccanaleassisi.com
- **Cuisine Type**: Umbrian and Mediterranean fusion
- **Average Meal Cost**: €25-40
- **Opening Hours**: 12:00 PM – 3:00 PM, 7:00 PM – 10:00 PM
- **Reservations**: Recommended
- **Specialties**: Porchetta, seafood risotto

Nestled near the Cathedral of San Rufino, **Il Baccanale** offers a delightful mix of Umbrian and Mediterranean flavors. I still remember their porchetta – the crackling skin and tender meat were heavenly. Their seafood risotto is another standout dish, rich in flavor and cooked to perfection. The staff is incredibly attentive, ensuring you feel right at home.

5. Locanda del Cardinale

- **Address**: Piazza del Vescovado, 8, Assisi
- **Contact**: +39 075 813620
- **Website**: www.locandadelcardinale.com
- **Cuisine Type**: Fine dining
- **Average Meal Cost**: €40-70

- **Opening Hours**: 12:30 PM – 2:30 PM, 7:30 PM – 10:30 PM
- **Reservations**: Highly recommended
- **Specialties**: Gourmet tasting menus, lamb with truffle

Dining at **Locanda del Cardinale** is a luxurious experience. The restaurant is built atop ancient Roman ruins, visible through the glass floors – a detail that adds a magical touch to the atmosphere. The lamb with truffle sauce was a highlight of my meal, perfectly tender and bursting with flavor. For a special occasion, this place is worth every euro.

6. Enoteca Mazzini

- **Address**: Corso Mazzini, 10, Assisi
- **Contact**: +39 075 8155033
- **Cuisine Type**: Wine bar with small plates
- **Average Meal Cost**: €15-30
- **Opening Hours**: 5:00 PM – 12:00 AM
- **Reservations**: Not usually required
- **Specialties**: Local wines, charcuterie boards, bruschetta

For wine lovers, **Enoteca Mazzini** is a hidden gem. This cozy wine bar offers an impressive selection of local wines paired with small plates like bruschetta and charcuterie. I spent an evening here sipping on a full-bodied Montefalco Rosso and nibbling on their creamy burrata with sun-dried tomatoes. It's a great spot to unwind after a day of exploring.

7. Ristorante La Fortezza

- **Address**: Via Porta Perlici, 27, Assisi

- **Contact**: +39 075 812204
- **Website**: www.ristorantelafortezza.com
- **Cuisine Type**: Traditional Umbrian
- **Average Meal Cost**: €20-35
- **Opening Hours**: 12:00 PM – 10:00 PM
- **Reservations**: Suggested for dinner
- **Specialties**: Wild boar ragu, tiramisu

Located near Rocca Maggiore, **Ristorante La Fortezza** combines stunning views with authentic flavors. Their wild boar ragu, served over handmade pappardelle, is hearty and satisfying. Save room for dessert – their tiramisu is a masterpiece of creamy layers and bold coffee flavor. The staff's warmth and the restaurant's medieval-inspired decor make the experience even more memorable.

8. Agriturismo Il Giardino dei Ciliegi

- **Address**: Via Petrata, 37, Assisi
- **Contact**: +39 075 815515
- **Website**: www.ilgiardinodeiciliegi.com
- **Cuisine Type**: Farm-to-table
- **Average Meal Cost**: €25-40
- **Opening Hours**: 1:00 PM – 3:00 PM, 7:00 PM – 9:30 PM
- **Reservations**: Necessary
- **Specialties**: Seasonal dishes, roasted lamb

For a true farm-to-table experience, **Agriturismo Il Giardino dei Ciliegi** is unparalleled. Set amidst the rolling hills outside Assisi, this family-run restaurant offers dishes made with ingredients grown on their farm. I fell in love with their roasted lamb, seasoned simply to let the natural flavors shine. Dining here feels like being welcomed into a family home.

9. Trattoria degli Umbri

- **Address**: Piazza del Comune, 40, Assisi
- **Contact**: +39 075 812455
- **Cuisine Type**: Traditional Umbrian
- **Average Meal Cost**: €20-35
- **Opening Hours**: 12:00 PM – 2:30 PM, 7:00 PM – 10:00 PM
- **Reservations**: Recommended
- **Specialties**: Strangozzi al tartufo, roasted lamb

Located right in the heart of Assisi at Piazza del Comune, **Trattoria degli Umbri** offers a cozy atmosphere with stone walls and a vaulted ceiling. The strangozzi al tartufo, a local pasta dish with truffles, is a must-try. The roasted lamb is tender and flavorful, reflecting the rich culinary traditions of the region. The friendly staff and quick service make dining here a delightful experience.

10. Osteria del Mulino

- **Address**: Via Ponte dei Galli, 1, Assisi
- **Contact**: +39 075 816831
- **Cuisine Type**: Rustic Italian
- **Average Meal Cost**: €25-40
- **Opening Hours**: 12:00 PM – 2:30 PM, 7:00 PM – 10:00 PM
- **Reservations**: Suggested
- **Specialties**: Rigatoni with white chianina ragout, black angus tagliata

Situated on the edge of Assisi in the leafy Bosco di San Francesco, **Osteria del Mulino** exudes rustic charm with its exposed beams and arched stone ceilings. The rigatoni with white chianina ragout is a hearty dish that showcases the quality of local beef. The black angus tagliata, seasoned with rosemary, is cooked to perfection. Dining here feels like a warm embrace from the Umbrian countryside.

11. Il Vicoletto

- **Address**: Vicolo dei Macelli Vecchi, 1, Assisi
- **Contact**: +39 075 813620
- **Cuisine Type**: Modern Umbrian
- **Average Meal Cost**: €30-50
- **Opening Hours**: 12:00 PM – 2:30 PM, 7:00 PM – 10:00 PM
- **Reservations**: Advised
- **Specialties**: Grilled octopus, homemade taglierini with quail eggs and truffles

Tucked away in a small alley near the Roman Forum, **Il Vicoletto** offers a modern twist on Umbrian classics. The grilled octopus is tender and flavorful, while the homemade taglierini with quail eggs and truffles is a delightful fusion of textures and tastes. The intimate setting, with its arched stone ceilings, adds to the charm of this hidden gem.

12. Hostaria Terra Chiama

- **Address**: Via San Rufino, 16, Assisi
- **Contact**: +39 075 812709
- **Cuisine Type**: Authentic Umbrian
- **Average Meal Cost**: €20-35
- **Opening Hours**: 12:00 PM – 2:30 PM, 7:00 PM – 10:00 PM

- **Reservations**: Recommended
- **Specialties**: Rabbit alla cacciatore, guinea fowl

Close to the cathedral and Piazza del Comune, **Hostaria Terra Chiama** serves authentic Umbrian dishes that highlight fresh, local produce. The rabbit alla cacciatore is rich with onions, tomatoes, and red wine, offering a true taste of the region. The guinea fowl is another specialty that showcases the restaurant's commitment to traditional flavors.

13. Benedikto

- **Address**: Via Eremo delle Carceri, 1A, Assisi
- **Contact**: +39 075 815515
- **Cuisine Type**: Contemporary Italian
- **Average Meal Cost**: €40-60
- **Opening Hours**: 7:30 PM – 10:30 PM
- **Reservations**: Necessary
- **Specialties**: Duck breast with red turnip sauce, salted codfish with green apple and lime

Located within the Nun Assisi Relais Spa Museum, **Benedikto** offers a contemporary dining experience with a menu that excites the senses. The duck breast served with red turnip sauce is a harmonious blend of flavors, while the salted codfish accompanied by green apple and lime provides a refreshing twist. The terrace offers stunning views of Assisi, enhancing the overall dining experience.

Exploring Street Food in Assisi: A Delightful Journey for Food Lovers

When you think of Assisi, the first thing that likely comes to mind is its rich history, breathtaking architecture, and the peaceful aura of Saint Francis of Assisi. But beyond its sacred spaces and historical significance, this charming Umbrian town offers another gem: its street food. Walking through its cobblestone streets, you can't help but be drawn to the tantalizing aromas wafting through the air. From traditional Umbrian dishes to quick bites perfect for exploring on the go, Assisi's street food scene is a treat for any traveler.

1. La Taverna di San Rufino

- **Vendor:** La Taverna di San Rufino
- **Location:** Piazza San Rufino
- **Operating Hours:** 10:00 AM – 8:00 PM
- **Specialty Dish:** Porchetta Panini
- **Average Cost:** €5
- **Must-Try:** Porchetta with Truffle Spread

Nestled near the stunning San Rufino Cathedral, this small stand offers one of the most iconic street foods in Assisi: *porchetta*. The first bite of their *porchetta panini* is unforgettable. The juicy, perfectly seasoned roast pork is sliced thin and layered into fresh bread. What sets this vendor apart is the option to add a truffle spread—a luxurious touch that elevates the simple sandwich into something extraordinary. I still remember sitting on a nearby bench, enjoying my panini while soaking in the cathedral's beauty.

2. Il Panaro dei Sapori

- **Vendor:** Il Panaro dei Sapori
- **Location:** Via San Francesco
- **Operating Hours:** 9:00 AM – 6:00 PM
- **Specialty Dish:** Torta al Testo
- **Average Cost:** €4-€6
- **Must-Try:** Prosciutto and Pecorino Torta al Testo

A trip to Assisi isn't complete without trying *torta al testo*, a type of flatbread native to Umbria. At Il Panaro dei Sapori, they take this traditional bread and fill it with a variety of ingredients. My favorite combination was prosciutto and pecorino cheese—simple yet bursting with flavor. Watching the staff grill the *torta al testo* on a hot plate made the experience even more authentic. The smoky aroma and the satisfying crunch of the bread left me craving more.

3. Antica Norcineria Umbra

- **Vendor:** Antica Norcineria Umbra
- **Location:** Piazza del Comune
- **Operating Hours:** 11:00 AM – 9:00 PM
- **Specialty Dish:** Salumi Platters
- **Average Cost:** €8
- **Must-Try:** Wild Boar Salami Sandwich

For lovers of cured meats, this is the place to be. The vendor specializes in *norcineria*, a tradition of crafting cured meats from the region. Their wild boar salami sandwich is rich and earthy, paired perfectly with a glass of Umbrian red wine. They also offer smaller snack options like *salumi* cones, which are great for munching on as you explore the nearby Piazza del Comune. I still remember the sharp, savory taste of the salami paired with the crunch of fresh bread—it was like a taste of Umbrian heritage.

4. Dolce Vita Gelateria

- **Vendor:** Dolce Vita Gelateria
- **Location:** Via Portica
- **Operating Hours:** 11:00 AM – 10:00 PM
- **Specialty Dish:** Gelato
- **Average Cost:** €3
- **Must-Try:** Pistachio and Stracciatella

After indulging in savory delights, nothing beats the cool, creamy sweetness of gelato. Dolce Vita Gelateria is a small spot that feels like a hidden treasure. Their pistachio gelato is hands-down the best I've ever tasted—rich, nutty, and not overly sweet. Paired with a scoop of *stracciatella* (vanilla gelato with chocolate shavings), it was a dessert worth savoring. I took mine in a cone and enjoyed it while strolling down the picturesque Via Portica.

5. Assisi Food Truck

- **Vendor:** Assisi Food Truck
- **Location:** Porta Nuova Parking Area
- **Operating Hours:** 12:00 PM – 9:00 PM
- **Specialty Dish:** Frittelle di Verdure
- **Average Cost:** €4
- **Must-Try:** Zucchini Fritters

Located conveniently near the Porta Nuova parking lot, this food truck is a lifesaver for anyone looking for a quick, affordable bite. Their *frittelle di verdure* (vegetable fritters) are light, crispy, and incredibly satisfying. I ordered a batch of zucchini fritters, freshly fried and sprinkled with a pinch of sea salt. They were the perfect snack to fuel my climb up to the Rocca Maggiore.

6. Piazza Santa Chiara Pasticceria Stand

- **Vendor:** Santa Chiara Pasticceria Stand
- **Location:** Piazza Santa Chiara
- **Operating Hours:** 8:00 AM – 7:00 PM
- **Specialty Dish:** Biscotti and Cantucci
- **Average Cost:** €3
- **Must-Try:** Almond Cantucci with Vin Santo

Right in front of the serene Basilica of Santa Chiara, this vendor offers delightful baked goods. Their almond *cantucci* (biscotti) paired with a small cup of *vin santo* (a sweet Italian dessert wine) was a revelation. Dunking the crunchy biscuit into the wine softened it perfectly, creating a harmonious blend of textures and flavors. It's an experience that felt quintessentially Italian.

7. Truffle & Cheese Stand

- **Vendor:** Truffle & Cheese Stand
- **Location:** Corso Mazzini
- **Operating Hours:** 10:00 AM – 6:00 PM
- **Specialty Dish:** Truffle Bruschetta
- **Average Cost:** €5
- **Must-Try:** Black Truffle and Ricotta Bruschetta

Corso Mazzini is home to this fantastic stand dedicated to the region's most prized ingredient: truffles. Their *truffle bruschetta* was heavenly—a warm slice of crusty bread topped with creamy ricotta and shaved black truffles. The earthy, aromatic truffles paired with the rich cheese created a bite I'll never forget. It's the kind of snack that makes you want to slow down and savor every moment.

8. La Piazzetta Food Cart

- **Vendor:** La Piazzetta Food Cart
- **Location:** Piazza Inferiore di San Francesco
- **Operating Hours:** 9:00 AM – 7:00 PM
- **Specialty Dish:** Arancini
- **Average Cost:** €3
- **Must-Try:** Saffron and Mozzarella Arancini

A stone's throw from the Basilica of San Francesco, La Piazzetta Food Cart offers the perfect pick-me-up: *arancini*. These golden-fried rice balls are crispy on the outside and creamy on the inside. My favorite was the saffron and mozzarella variety, which had a rich, buttery flavor. Holding one in hand while gazing at the basilica felt like the perfect fusion of food and culture.

9. Piadina e Sapori

- **Vendor:** Piadina e Sapori
- **Location:** Via Borgo Aretino
- **Operating Hours:** 11:30 AM – 9:00 PM
- **Specialty Dish:** Piadina with Sausage and Greens
- **Average Cost:** €6
- **Must-Try:** Piadina with Sausage, Arugula, and Pecorino

If you're a fan of flatbreads, make your way to Piadina e Sapori. Their piadina (a thin Italian flatbread) stuffed with sausage, fresh arugula, and shaved pecorino cheese is a local favorite. The bread is warm and slightly charred, and the filling is both hearty and fresh. It's an ideal snack to enjoy while wandering through the quieter streets of Assisi.

10. Gelato Artigianale San Damiano

- **Vendor:** Gelato Artigianale San Damiano
- **Location:** Near the Church of San Damiano
- **Operating Hours:** 12:00 PM – 8:00 PM
- **Specialty Dish:** Fig and Honey Gelato
- **Average Cost:** €3
- **Must-Try:** Fig and Honey Gelato

End your street food tour with a sweet treat from this artisanal gelato stand near the Church of San Damiano. The fig and honey gelato is a flavor you won't find everywhere, and it captures the essence of Umbrian produce. Creamy, fragrant, and perfectly balanced, it was the ideal way to wrap up my Assisi street food adventure.

11. Forno di Francesco

- **Vendor:** Forno di Francesco
- **Location:** Via San Rufino, near the Cathedral
- **Operating Hours:** 8:00 AM – 6:00 PM
- **Specialty Dish:** Pizza Bianca with Rosemary
- **Average Cost:** €2 per slice
- **Must-Try:** Pizza Bianca with Olive Oil and Sea Salt

This tiny bakery, named after Saint Francis, offers the most aromatic and flavorful *pizza bianca* (white pizza) I've ever tasted. It's a simple yet addictive combination of olive oil, fresh rosemary, and sea salt baked onto a thin, crispy crust. The slices are cut generously, making it a perfect snack for strolling through Assisi's historical streets. Pair it with a cup of their freshly squeezed orange juice for an energizing treat.

12. Osteria in Strada

- **Vendor:** Osteria in Strada
- **Location:** Piazza Matteotti
- **Operating Hours:** 10:00 AM – 9:00 PM
- **Specialty Dish:** Polpette (Meatballs)
- **Average Cost:** €6
- **Must-Try:** Lamb Meatballs with Tomato Sauce

Right by one of Assisi's main bus stops, Osteria in Strada is a humble stall serving up rich, hearty flavors. Their lamb meatballs, cooked in a tangy tomato sauce, are tender and packed with herbs. Served in a small container with a slice of bread to soak up the sauce, this dish is both filling and flavorful. I had mine while waiting for a bus to nearby Perugia, and it felt like a warm, comforting hug in food form.

13. La Carrettiera

- **Vendor:** La Carrettiera
- **Location:** Via Fontebella
- **Operating Hours:** 12:00 PM – 8:00 PM
- **Specialty Dish:** Stuffed Olives (Olive Ascolane)
- **Average Cost:** €5 for six olives
- **Must-Try:** Olive Ascolane with Pork Filling

La Carrettiera specializes in *olive ascolane*, a delicacy from nearby Marche that has become a favorite in Assisi. These large green olives are stuffed with a seasoned pork mixture, coated in breadcrumbs, and fried until golden brown. Served hot, they're crispy on the outside and bursting with savory goodness on the inside. I enjoyed these while walking along the picturesque Via Fontebella, marveling at the stunning views of the Umbrian valley.

14. I Sapori di Assisi

- **Vendor:** I Sapori di Assisi
- **Location:** Corso Mazzini
- **Operating Hours:** 9:00 AM – 7:00 PM
- **Specialty Dish:** Pecorino and Honey Crostini
- **Average Cost:** €4
- **Must-Try:** Aged Pecorino with Chestnut Honey

This small cart is an homage to Umbrian flavors, showcasing local cheeses and honey in bite-sized crostini. My favorite was the aged pecorino paired with chestnut honey, offering a perfect blend of sharp, creamy, and sweet flavors. It was a delight to stand there, sampling different combinations while chatting with the vendor, who was eager to share the stories behind the ingredients.

15. Angolo delle Frittelle

- **Vendor:** Angolo delle Frittelle
- **Location:** Piazza San Pietro
- **Operating Hours:** 11:00 AM – 10:00 PM
- **Specialty Dish:** Sweet Fritters with Raisins
- **Average Cost:** €3 for a bag
- **Must-Try:** Fritters with Raisins and Lemon Zest

Just outside the Basilica of San Pietro, this cozy stand specializes in *frittelle*, a type of Italian fritter. The sweet variety, studded with raisins and a hint of lemon zest, is an absolute treat. Light and fluffy, they're sprinkled with powdered sugar and served warm in a paper bag. I grabbed a bag and shared it with fellow travelers, making it a memorable moment of shared joy.

16. Panino del Pellegrino

- **Vendor:** Panino del Pellegrino
- **Location:** Via Cardinale Raffaele Merry del Val
- **Operating Hours:** 10:00 AM – 6:00 PM
- **Specialty Dish:** Panino with Truffle Sausage
- **Average Cost:** €7
- **Must-Try:** Truffle Sausage and Arugula Panino

Aimed at pilgrims visiting Assisi, this vendor creates hearty sandwiches to keep you energized throughout your journey. Their truffle sausage panino, paired with fresh arugula and a drizzle of olive oil, is the ultimate flavor bomb. The combination of earthy truffles and spicy sausage is so satisfying, I couldn't help but grab another for the road.

17. Frutta Fresca Assisi

- **Vendor:** Frutta Fresca Assisi
- **Location:** Piazza del Comune
- **Operating Hours:** 8:00 AM – 4:00 PM
- **Specialty Dish:** Seasonal Fruit Cups
- **Average Cost:** €3
- **Must-Try:** Fresh Figs and Grapes

Amidst all the rich flavors of Assisi's street food, sometimes a refreshing fruit cup is exactly what you need. This small vendor near the lively Piazza del Comune offers cups filled with seasonal fruits, like juicy figs, sweet grapes, and crisp apples. It's a light and healthy option that pairs perfectly with a day of sightseeing.

18. Sagra della Bruschetta

- **Vendor:** Sagra della Bruschetta
- **Location:** Seasonal Pop-Up Stand in Piazza Santa Chiara
- **Operating Hours:** 10:00 AM – 8:00 PM (seasonal)
- **Specialty Dish:** Bruschetta al Pomodoro
- **Average Cost:** €2.50 per slice
- **Must-Try:** Tomato and Basil Bruschetta

If you visit Assisi during one of its seasonal festivals, don't miss the chance to try the *bruschetta* from this pop-up vendor. Made with freshly baked bread, ripe tomatoes, fragrant basil, and a drizzle of the region's renowned olive oil, it's a simple yet exquisite snack. I tried one during a summer festival and was amazed at how such humble ingredients could pack such vibrant flavor.

19. Vinoteca Mobile

- **Vendor:** Vinoteca Mobile
- **Location:** Various locations, often near Rocca Maggiore
- **Operating Hours:** 12:00 PM – 8:00 PM
- **Specialty Dish:** Wine Slushies
- **Average Cost:** €4
- **Must-Try:** White Wine Slushy with Lemon

This mobile wine bar adds a unique twist to the street food scene by offering *wine slushies*. The white wine slushy with a hint of lemon is incredibly refreshing, especially on a warm day. Sipping this icy treat while overlooking the panoramic views from Rocca Maggiore is an experience I still daydream about.

20. Creperia Umbra

- **Vendor:** Creperia Umbra
- **Location:** Via Borgo Aretino
- **Operating Hours:** 11:00 AM – 10:00 PM
- **Specialty Dish:** Nutella Crepes
- **Average Cost:** €4
- **Must-Try:** Crepes with Nutella and Chopped Hazelnuts

For those with a sweet tooth, Creperia Umbra serves up irresistible crepes. Their Nutella crepe, topped with a generous sprinkle of chopped hazelnuts, is rich and decadent. Watching the crepes being freshly prepared adds to the charm, and it's a perfect snack to end a day of exploring Assisi's treasures.

Food Markets in Assisi

When wandering through the charming streets of Assisi, one of the most delightful ways to immerse yourself in the culture is by exploring its vibrant food markets. Whether you're a passionate foodie or a casual traveler with a love for authentic experiences, these markets are a window into the heart of Umbrian life. From locally grown produce to handcrafted delicacies, every stall tells a story. Here's my personal take on the best food markets in Assisi, based on experiences that left me both well-fed and deeply connected to the region.

Mercato della Piazza del Comune

- **Location**: Piazza del Comune, Assisi
- **Operating Days**: Tuesday and Saturday
- **Operating Hours**: 7:00 AM – 1:30 PM
- **Specialties**: Fresh produce, artisanal cheeses, baked goods, and seasonal truffles
- **Average Price Range**: €5-€25 depending on the item

If there's one market that feels like the beating heart of Assisi, it's the **Mercato della Piazza del Comune**. Located right in the center of town, this market combines the charm of a historical setting with the hustle and bustle of local vendors. I remember arriving early one Tuesday morning, greeted by the scent of freshly baked *pane di Assisi* and the rich aroma of roasted coffee wafting from nearby cafés.

The seasonal produce here is incredible. During my visit in the autumn, I found myself marveling at the array of truffles—those earthy treasures that Umbrian cuisine is famous for. The vendors, always enthusiastic about their craft, were more than happy to let me sample their *pecorino cheese* paired with a drizzle of local honey. My tip? Don't hesitate to strike up a conversation—many vendors are happy to share cooking tips or even recommend recipes.

For bargain hunters, try bundling items for a better deal. I managed to snag a trio of cheeses and a loaf of *rosmarino focaccia* for under €15 after a friendly chat with the vendor.

Mercato delle Erbe

- **Location**: Via San Francesco, Assisi
- **Operating Days**: Wednesday and Saturday

- **Operating Hours**: 8:00 AM – 2:00 PM
- **Specialties**: Fresh herbs, spices, organic fruits, and vegetables
- **Average Price Range**: €3-€15 per bundle

Nestled in a quieter corner of Assisi, the **Mercato delle Erbe** is a hidden gem that I stumbled upon while exploring the path to the Basilica of St. Francis. This market is smaller than some of the others, but its charm lies in its focus on fresh herbs and organic produce.

Walking through the stalls felt like stepping into a fragrant garden. Basil, rosemary, sage, and thyme spilled out of every corner, their aromas mingling in the crisp morning air. I couldn't resist buying a bundle of sage, which I later used to make a simple *burro e salvia* pasta at my Airbnb. The vendors here often grow their produce in small family gardens, making everything feel even more special.

A little tip: if you're buying larger quantities or multiple bundles of herbs, don't be shy about asking for a discount. The vendors here are kind and approachable, especially if you show genuine interest in their produce.

Mercato di Porta Nuova

- **Location**: Porta Nuova, Assisi
- **Operating Days**: Friday
- **Operating Hours**: 7:30 AM – 1:00 PM
- **Specialties**: Cured meats, olive oil, wine, and baked goods
- **Average Price Range**: €7-€30 depending on the product

If you're staying near the eastern side of Assisi, the **Mercato di Porta Nuova** is an unmissable stop for food lovers. This market has a reputation for its selection of cured meats and olive oils, two staples of Umbrian cuisine. I still remember sampling slices of *prosciutto di Norcia* from a vendor who sliced it paper-thin right before my eyes.

The olive oils here are exceptional. Vendors often offer tastings, where you can dip pieces of crusty bread into oils ranging from delicate to robust. I ended up buying a small bottle of peppery extra virgin olive oil for about €12—a purchase that instantly elevated my home-cooked meals.

Another highlight of this market is the freshly baked *tozzetti* (Umbrian biscotti). Perfect with a cup of coffee or as a souvenir, these cookies are a must-try. Don't forget to ask vendors about their homemade wine selections; I was introduced to a delightful bottle of *Sagrantino di Montefalco* that became the highlight of my dinner later that evening.

Mercatino del Contadino

- **Location**: Piazza Santa Chiara, Assisi
- **Operating Days**: Monday and Thursday
- **Operating Hours**: 8:00 AM – 12:30 PM
- **Specialties**: Organic honey, jams, and farm-fresh eggs
- **Average Price Range**: €2-€10

For a truly local experience, the **Mercatino del Contadino** offers a chance to interact with Assisi's small-scale farmers. Located near the serene Piazza Santa Chiara, this market specializes in farm-fresh products that feel straight out of the countryside.

One of my favorite purchases here was a jar of wildflower honey. The vendor, a kind elderly man named Giovanni, explained how his bees forage in the nearby hills, resulting in honey with a unique floral flavor. It paired wonderfully with the *pecorino* I bought at another market.

This market is also a great place to pick up jams made from seasonal fruits. During my visit in the summer, I discovered an incredible apricot jam that tasted like sunshine in a jar. If you're staying in Assisi for a few days and have access to a kitchen, don't miss the chance to grab some farm-fresh eggs—they make for the fluffiest omelets!

Mercato delle Spezie

- **Location**: Via Fontebella, Assisi
- **Operating Days**: Saturday
- **Operating Hours**: 9:00 AM – 1:00 PM
- **Specialties**: Spices, dried mushrooms, and truffle products
- **Average Price Range**: €5-€20

As a lover of bold flavors, I couldn't resist visiting the **Mercato delle Spezie**. This market is a treasure trove for anyone who loves cooking with spices and specialty ingredients. From saffron to dried porcini mushrooms, every stall seemed to offer something exotic yet quintessentially Umbrian.

I was particularly drawn to the truffle products. Small jars of truffle-infused butter and truffle salt were among the highlights, and the vendors were generous with samples. I couldn't resist picking up a jar of black truffle paste for about €15—a splurge, but worth every penny.

For spice lovers, the paprika and chili blends are excellent finds. I also recommend buying a small packet of *finocchietto selvatico* (wild fennel), which is often used in traditional Umbrian sausages. My advice? Take your time to explore and let the vendors guide you—they often have the best tips for using their products in simple, flavorful dishes.

Tips for Visiting Assisi's Food Markets

1. **Arrive Early**: Many markets in Assisi start winding down by early afternoon, so it's best to arrive early for the freshest picks.
2. **Bring Cash**: While some vendors accept cards, cash is preferred—and it's easier to negotiate prices this way.
3. **Taste Before You Buy**: Most vendors are happy to offer samples, so don't hesitate to try before making a purchase.
4. **Bring a Bag**: Eco-conscious travelers will appreciate having a reusable shopping bag handy, as many vendors don't provide bags.
5. **Engage with the Vendors**: A little Italian goes a long way! Even simple phrases like *"Quanto costa?"* (How much?) or *"Grazie!"* (Thank you) can create a more enjoyable interaction.

Bars and Pubs in Assisi

Nestled in the heart of Italy's Umbria region, Assisi is renowned for its historical and spiritual significance, but the town also boasts a delightful selection of bars and pubs. These establishments are perfect for unwinding after a day of exploring the stunning basilicas, cobblestone streets, and hilltop vistas. Let me take you through some of the must-visit spots, where I've sipped aperitivos and mingled with locals during my time in this enchanting town.

Bar Trovadores

- **Address**: Piazza del Comune, Assisi, Italy
- **Contact**: +39 075 812345
- **Website**: www.bartrovadoresassisi.com
- **Specialty Drinks**: Aperol Spritz, Negroni, and local Umbrian wines
- **Happy Hour**: 6:00 PM to 8:00 PM – enjoy complimentary snacks with your drinks
- **Entertainment**: Occasional live acoustic music on weekends
- **Opening Hours**: 10:00 AM – 11:00 PM

Bar Trovadores is one of those places that feels effortlessly authentic. Located right in the bustling Piazza del Comune, it offers prime people-watching opportunities. On my visit, I found a charming mix of locals catching up over espresso and tourists marveling at the medieval architecture while sipping cocktails. Their Aperol Spritz was perfectly balanced, and the complimentary bruschetta during happy hour was a delightful touch. On Fridays, they host live acoustic sets, making it a cozy spot to soak in some local talent.

La Taverna del Vino

- **Address**: Via Portica, 25, Assisi, Italy
- **Contact**: +39 075 813567
- **Website**: www.latavernadelvinoassisi.com
- **Specialty Drinks**: Selection of fine Umbrian wines and craft beers
- **Happy Hour**: 5:30 PM to 7:30 PM – discounted glasses of wine and charcuterie boards
- **Entertainment**: Wine tastings and pairing sessions
- **Opening Hours**: 12:00 PM – 10:00 PM

This cozy wine bar tucked away on a narrow street is a gem for wine enthusiasts. The sommelier here, Marco, guided me through their impressive selection of Umbrian wines, from the robust Montefalco Rosso to the crisp Grechetto. I couldn't resist pairing a glass with their cheese and salami board, which features local delicacies. If you visit, try their wine tasting experience – it's an intimate way to learn about Umbrian viticulture.

Caffè Minerva

- **Address**: Corso Mazzini, 12, Assisi, Italy
- **Contact**: +39 075 814321
- **Website**: www.caffeminervaassisi.com
- **Specialty Drinks**: Espresso martini, signature Minerva Mojito
- **Happy Hour**: 6:00 PM to 9:00 PM – half-price cocktails
- **Entertainment**: Weekly trivia nights and occasional karaoke
- **Opening Hours**: 8:00 AM – Midnight

Caffè Minerva is a modern yet inviting spot that effortlessly blends café culture with nightlife. I stumbled upon this place during a leisurely evening stroll and was drawn in by its vibrant energy. Their signature mojito had a refreshing twist with hints of basil, and the atmosphere was lively but never overwhelming. If you're a trivia buff, drop by on Thursdays to join in their fun and competitive quiz nights.

Bar degli Artisti

- **Address**: Via San Francesco, 15, Assisi, Italy
- **Contact**: +39 075 819876

- **Website**: www.bardegliartistiassisi.com
- **Specialty Drinks**: Classic Bellini, Umbrian herbal liquors
- **Happy Hour**: 4:00 PM to 7:00 PM – discounts on cocktails and small plates
- **Entertainment**: Art displays and occasional live poetry readings
- **Opening Hours**: 11:00 AM – 11:00 PM

Art and culture aficionados will feel right at home at Bar degli Artisti. This bar serves as a meeting point for creative souls and often features local artists' work on its walls. I was lucky to attend one of their live poetry nights, and the intimate setting added to the charm. Their Bellini, made with fresh peach purée, was a highlight for me.

Pub San Rufino

- **Address**: Via Anfiteatro Romano, 9, Assisi, Italy
- **Contact**: +39 075 820123
- **Website**: www.pubsanrufinoassisi.com
- **Specialty Drinks**: Craft beers and Umbrian cider
- **Happy Hour**: 6:00 PM to 8:00 PM – discounted pints and nibbles
- **Entertainment**: Sports screenings and live rock bands
- **Opening Hours**: 5:00 PM – 1:00 AM

For a more laid-back vibe, Pub San Rufino is your go-to. This place has a robust selection of Italian craft beers, and their Umbrian cider was a pleasant surprise – tart, refreshing, and perfect for a summer evening. The staff is friendly and eager to share their recommendations. During my visit, they had a local rock band playing, which added an energetic buzz to the night.

L'Angolo dei Sapori

- **Address**: Via Carducci, 7, Assisi, Italy
- **Contact**: +39 075 822345
- **Website**: www.langolodeisaporiassisi.com
- **Specialty Drinks**: Sangria and Umbrian craft gin cocktails
- **Happy Hour**: 5:30 PM to 7:30 PM – tapas and cocktails combo
- **Entertainment**: Outdoor seating with scenic views, occasional live DJs
- **Opening Hours**: 3:00 PM – 11:00 PM

L'Angolo dei Sapori is perfect for those looking for a mix of great drinks and spectacular views. Perched on a hill, this bar offers panoramic vistas of Assisi's countryside. I sipped on their Umbrian gin and tonic as the sun dipped below the horizon – a truly magical experience. Their sangria, infused with local fruits, is another must-try.

Bar Rocca Maggiore

- **Address**: Via della Rocca, 2, Assisi, Italy
- **Contact**: +39 075 823456
- **Website**: www.barroccamaggioreassisi.com
- **Specialty Drinks**: Limoncello Spritz, Umbrian white wine
- **Happy Hour**: 4:30 PM to 7:00 PM – cocktails with complimentary appetizers
- **Entertainment**: Stunning rooftop views and jazz evenings
- **Opening Hours**: 12:00 PM – 10:30 PM

Set near Assisi's iconic Rocca Maggiore fortress, this bar offers an unforgettable experience. The rooftop terrace is the star here, providing sweeping views of the town's terracotta rooftops and surrounding hills. On jazz nights, the soulful music perfectly complements the romantic ambiance. Their Limoncello Spritz is light, zesty, and an absolute delight.

Enoteca La Divina

- **Address**: Via Santa Chiara, 5, Assisi, Italy
- **Contact**: +39 075 817654
- **Website**: www.enotecaladivinaassisi.com
- **Specialty Drinks**: Montefalco Sagrantino, Prosecco flights
- **Happy Hour**: 6:00 PM to 8:00 PM – half-price wine tastings and appetizers
- **Entertainment**: Wine and cheese pairing workshops
- **Opening Hours**: 12:00 PM – 10:00 PM

Enoteca La Divina is a wine lover's paradise. Tucked near the Basilica of Santa Chiara, it offers a curated selection of local and national wines. Their Montefalco Sagrantino left me absolutely floored with its rich, velvety notes. Pairing it with their pecorino cheese was divine, and their Prosecco flights were bubbly perfection. If you're curious about Umbrian wines, the sommelier-led workshops here are worth attending.

Bar Perugia

- **Address**: Piazza San Francesco, 2, Assisi, Italy
- **Contact**: +39 075 815432
- **Website**: www.barperugiaassisi.com
- **Specialty Drinks**: Assisi Mule (a local take on the Moscow Mule)
- **Happy Hour**: 5:30 PM to 7:30 PM – 2-for-1 cocktails
- **Entertainment**: Street performers and live acoustic music
- **Opening Hours**: 9:00 AM – 11:00 PM

Bar Perugia is ideally located in Piazza San Francesco, offering front-row views of the basilica and a lively square. Their Assisi Mule, crafted with a hint of Umbrian ginger, was refreshing and unique. I loved relaxing on their outdoor terrace while listening to street performers who added a vibrant touch to the evening. Don't miss their happy hour—it's a steal!

La Birreria Umbra

- **Address**: Via San Rufino, 8, Assisi, Italy
- **Contact**: +39 075 821234
- **Website**: www.labirreriaumbraassisi.com
- **Specialty Drinks**: Local craft beers, including Umbrian pale ales and stouts
- **Happy Hour**: 5:00 PM to 7:00 PM – discounted pints and Umbrian snacks
- **Entertainment**: Trivia nights and sports screenings
- **Opening Hours**: 3:00 PM – Midnight

Beer enthusiasts will love La Birreria Umbra, a rustic pub showcasing the best of local brewing. Their pale ale had subtle citrusy notes that paired perfectly with their olive and cheese platter. I attended one of their trivia nights—it was lively and fun, with locals and tourists mingling over pints. If you're into beer culture, this place is a must-visit.

Bar Vista Assisi

- **Address**: Via San Giacomo, 3, Assisi, Italy
- **Contact**: +39 075 824567
- **Website**: www.barvistaassisi.com
- **Specialty Drinks**: Aperol Granita and Umbrian herbal teas

- **Happy Hour**: 6:00 PM to 8:00 PM – cocktails with complimentary bruschetta
- **Entertainment**: Rooftop seating with live jazz evenings
- **Opening Hours**: 11:00 AM – Midnight

Bar Vista Assisi offers breathtaking views of the town's rolling hills. Their Aperol Granita was a refreshing twist on the classic aperitivo, and the rooftop seating made it an unforgettable experience. I visited during a jazz evening, and the music, coupled with the sunset view, was pure magic. It's an ideal spot for a romantic night out or a relaxed evening with friends.

Il Cantuccio

- **Address**: Via Arnaldo Fortini, 10, Assisi, Italy
- **Contact**: +39 075 812678
- **Website**: www.ilcantuccioassisi.com
- **Specialty Drinks**: Classic Italian cocktails and limoncello martinis
- **Happy Hour**: 5:00 PM to 7:00 PM – half-price cocktails with small bites
- **Entertainment**: DJ sets on weekends
- **Opening Hours**: 4:00 PM – 1:00 AM

Il Cantuccio brings a modern vibe to Assisi's traditional charm. Their limoncello martini was one of the best cocktails I've ever tasted—zesty and perfectly balanced. I visited on a Saturday night and enjoyed their DJ's upbeat playlist, which created a lively yet sophisticated atmosphere. If you're looking for a more contemporary bar experience in Assisi, this is the place.

Bar Le Fonti

- **Address**: Via Fontebella, 4, Assisi, Italy
- **Contact**: +39 075 823789
- **Website**: www.barlefontiassisi.com
- **Specialty Drinks**: Negroni Sbagliato and seasonal fruit cocktails
- **Happy Hour**: 6:00 PM to 9:00 PM – cocktails with fresh Umbrian produce
- **Entertainment**: Outdoor garden seating with fairy lights
- **Opening Hours**: 3:00 PM – Midnight

Bar Le Fonti feels like a hidden oasis in Assisi. Its garden seating, adorned with twinkling fairy lights, sets the stage for a magical evening. Their Negroni Sbagliato, made with prosecco instead of gin, was a delightful variation on the classic. I enjoyed the serene ambiance, sipping cocktails while surrounded by the gentle hum of conversation.

Vinoteca del Corso

- **Address**: Corso Mazzini, 14, Assisi, Italy
- **Contact**: +39 075 817234
- **Website**: www.vinotecadelcorsoassisi.com
- **Specialty Drinks**: Organic wines from Umbrian vineyards
- **Happy Hour**: 5:30 PM to 7:30 PM – wine flights and antipasto plates
- **Entertainment**: Wine tastings and live classical guitar performances
- **Opening Hours**: 11:00 AM – 10:00 PM

Vinoteca del Corso is a sophisticated spot for wine lovers. I was captivated by their selection of organic wines, particularly the Grechetto, which was crisp and refreshing. Their wine flights are a fantastic way to sample the region's best, and the live classical guitar performances create an elegant, calming backdrop.

L'Emporio del Vino

- **Address**: Via Fontebella, 22, Assisi, Italy
- **Contact**: +39 075 821345
- **Website**: www.lemporiodelvinoassisi.com
- **Specialty Drinks**: Rosé Spritz and handcrafted Vermouth cocktails
- **Happy Hour**: 6:00 PM to 8:00 PM – artisan cocktails with Umbrian olives
- **Entertainment**: Cocktail-making classes and storytelling nights
- **Opening Hours**: 12:00 PM – 11:00 PM

L'Emporio del Vino offers a unique twist on classic Italian cocktails. Their Rosé Spritz was light and fragrant, and their handcrafted Vermouth cocktails were bursting with flavor. I loved attending one of their storytelling nights, where locals shared legends of Assisi over drinks it was both entertaining and heartwarming.

Nightclubs in Assisi

Assisi, primarily known for its rich history and spiritual significance, may not immediately strike you as a nightlife hub. However, the charming town hides a few gems that come alive when the sun sets, offering visitors a unique blend of history, culture, and modern revelry. Whether you're a local looking for a lively night or a traveler seeking a fresh perspective on Assisi after dark, these nightclubs will leave you pleasantly surprised. Let's dive into the vibrant after-hours scene of this historic Italian town.

Club: Taverna della Luna

- **Address:** Via San Rufino, 15, Assisi, Italy
- **Contact:** +39 075 812345
- **Website:** www.tavernadellaluna.com
- **Entry Fee:** €10, includes a welcome drink
- **Theme Nights:** Retro Thursdays, Jazz Fridays
- **Opening Hours:** 9:00 PM - 2:00 AM
- **Age Restrictions:** 18+

When I first stepped into Taverna della Luna, I felt like I had been transported to a different era. Housed in a centuries-old stone building, the club beautifully blends Assisi's historic charm with a modern nightlife vibe. Retro Thursdays are an absolute treat, where locals and visitors groove to hits from the '70s and '80s. On Fridays, the club transforms into a haven for jazz lovers, with live bands that captivate the audience.

If you're visiting, try their signature drink, **Luna Spritz**, a delightful twist on the classic Aperol Spritz. The cozy ambiance, friendly crowd, and soulful music make it an unforgettable experience. Pro tip: Arrive early on jazz nights to grab a good spot near the stage.

Club: La Grotta Notturna

- **Address:** Piazza del Comune, 8, Assisi, Italy
- **Contact:** +39 075 825678
- **Website:** www.lagrottanotturna.com

- **Entry Fee:** €15, includes access to the rooftop lounge
- **Theme Nights:** Silent Disco Saturdays
- **Opening Hours:** 10:00 PM - 3:00 AM
- **Age Restrictions:** 21+

La Grotta Notturna is a literal underground marvel! As its name suggests, this nightclub is carved into the side of a hill, creating an intimate, cave-like setting. The acoustics here are incredible, making every beat resonate through your body. The highlight of my visit was their **Silent Disco Saturdays**. Imagine dancing in a room full of people, each immersed in their own vibe, headphones glowing in different colors—it's surreal and exhilarating.

The club also boasts a rooftop lounge that offers breathtaking views of Assisi's twinkling lights at night. It's the perfect spot for a breather before diving back into the pulsating beats. Don't forget to try their **Limoncello Martini**—it's as refreshing as it sounds!

Club: Palazzo Beat

- **Address:** Corso Mazzini, 25, Assisi, Italy
- **Contact:** +39 075 813456
- **Website:** www.palazzobeat.com
- **Entry Fee:** €20, includes two drinks
- **Theme Nights:** Latin Nights on Wednesdays, Electro Saturdays
- **Opening Hours:** 10:30 PM - 4:00 AM
- **Age Restrictions:** 18+

If you're in the mood for high-energy dancing, Palazzo Beat is where you need to be. Located in a renovated Renaissance-era palazzo, this club offers a stunning mix of historic architecture and modern lighting effects. The vibe here is electric, with DJs spinning everything from reggaeton to EDM.

I attended their **Latin Night**, and it was nothing short of spectacular. The dance floor was alive with people salsa-ing and bachata-ing the night away. The staff even offered free mini dance lessons for beginners, which was a thoughtful touch. Their **Palazzo Passionfruit Mojito** became my drink of choice for the night. The crowd here skews younger, but everyone is welcoming and ready to have a good time.

Club: Terra Disco Club

- **Address:** Via Los Angeles, 89, Assisi, Italy
- **Contact:** +39 075 817234
- **Website:** www.terradiscoclub.com
- **Entry Fee:** €12, includes a free shot
- **Theme Nights:** Ladies' Night Thursdays
- **Opening Hours:** 9:00 PM - 3:00 AM
- **Age Restrictions:** 18+

Terra Disco Club is perfect for those who love to party with a local crowd. Located just outside the city center, the club is known for its vibrant atmosphere and affordable prices. The DJ lineup here never disappoints, playing a mix of Italian pop, international hits, and house music.

The **Ladies' Night** on Thursdays is particularly popular—women enter for free and receive complimentary cocktails until 11 PM. The dance floor gets packed quickly, so make sure to arrive early. I spent most of my night sipping on their signature **Terra Tonic**, a refreshing gin-based concoction, and soaking in the lively energy of the place.

Club: Assisi Lounge Nights

- **Address:** Via Portica, 3, Assisi, Italy
- **Contact:** +39 075 819999
- **Website:** www.assisiloungenights.com
- **Entry Fee:** €18
- **Theme Nights:** Karaoke Thursdays, Chill Sundays
- **Opening Hours:** 8:00 PM - 1:00 AM
- **Age Restrictions:** 21+

For those looking for a more laid-back nightlife experience, Assisi Lounge Nights is the ideal spot. The club exudes elegance, with plush seating and ambient lighting that creates a relaxed atmosphere. On **Karaoke Thursdays**, the lounge becomes a stage for budding performers and enthusiastic amateurs alike. I couldn't resist belting out a classic Italian ballad, encouraged by the warm applause of the crowd.

Their **Chill Sundays** feature acoustic performances by local artists, making it a great place to unwind after a weekend of sightseeing. The menu here is also a highlight; their **Aperitivo Platter** paired with a glass of Chianti is a must-try.

Club: Mystica Underground

- **Address:** Via Fontebella, 45, Assisi, Italy
- **Contact:** +39 075 812678
- **Website:** www.mysticaunderground.com
- **Entry Fee:** €10
- **Theme Nights:** EDM Fridays
- **Opening Hours:** 10:00 PM - 4:00 AM
- **Age Restrictions:** 18+

Mystica Underground is the heartbeat of Assisi's electronic dance music scene. Tucked away in a discreet alley, this club draws a loyal crowd of EDM enthusiasts and party-goers. The vibe here is edgy, with neon-lit walls and an immersive sound system that keeps the energy levels sky-high.

On **EDM Fridays**, internationally acclaimed DJs take over the decks, spinning tracks that keep the crowd dancing until the early hours. I couldn't help but get lost in the pulsating beats and vibrant light displays. Their **Neon Shot Platter**, a colorful array of flavored shots, adds an extra spark to the evening.

Club: Velvet Groove

- **Address:** Via San Francesco, 12, Assisi, Italy
- **Contact:** +39 075 824567
- **Website:** www.velvetgroove.com
- **Entry Fee:** €15, includes a drink of choice
- **Theme Nights:** 80s Throwback Tuesdays, DJ Collab Nights
- **Opening Hours:** 9:30 PM - 2:30 AM
- **Age Restrictions:** 18+

Velvet Groove is a cozy, upscale club located near the Basilica of St. Francis. Despite its small size, the club has a loyal following thanks to its carefully curated theme nights and intimate vibe. I visited on **DJ Collab Night**, where two local DJs teamed up to create an unforgettable fusion of beats that had the entire crowd moving in sync.

Their **80s Throwback Tuesdays** are another highlight, where you can dance to Madonna, Queen, and Italian disco classics under a sparkling disco ball. Don't leave without trying their **Velvet Cosmopolitan**, a luxurious twist on the traditional cocktail.

Club: Il Ritmo Segreto

- **Address:** Via del Torrione, 6, Assisi, Italy
- **Contact:** +39 075 818910
- **Website:** www.ilritmosegreto.com
- **Entry Fee:** €10
- **Theme Nights:** Underground Beats Wednesdays
- **Opening Hours:** 10:00 PM - 3:00 AM
- **Age Restrictions:** 18+

If you love underground music and a more relaxed crowd, **Il Ritmo Segreto** (The Secret Rhythm) is the place to be. Hidden in a quiet part of town, the club boasts a minimalist design with dim lighting and a stellar sound system.

I attended their **Underground Beats Wednesday**, where indie and techno tracks dominated the night. It felt exclusive, almost like a secret party among friends. Their **Signature Espresso Martini** is the perfect pick-me-up after hours of dancing.

Club: Nero Notte

- **Address:** Corso Giuseppe Mazzini, 45, Assisi, Italy
- **Contact:** +39 075 813112
- **Website:** www.neronotteclub.com
- **Entry Fee:** €20, includes a welcome cocktail
- **Theme Nights:** Black & Gold Saturdays
- **Opening Hours:** 11:00 PM - 4:00 AM
- **Age Restrictions:** 21+

For a luxurious and glamorous experience, **Nero Notte** (Black Night) is unmatched. This nightclub caters to a sophisticated crowd, offering high-end cocktails and a meticulously designed space with gold accents and sleek black interiors.

Their **Black & Gold Saturdays** are a spectacle, featuring live performances, acrobatic dancers, and a curated DJ lineup. I felt like I was attending a VIP event, and the energy was nothing short of exhilarating. Make sure to sample their **Gold Rush Margarita**—it's a signature cocktail that matches the club's elegant theme.

Club: Disco da Vinci

- **Address:** Piazza Santa Chiara, 22, Assisi, Italy
- **Contact:** +39 075 827654
- **Website:** www.discodavinci.com
- **Entry Fee:** €12
- **Theme Nights:** Art Pop Thursdays
- **Opening Hours:** 9:00 PM - 3:00 AM
- **Age Restrictions:** 18+

Disco da Vinci is an eclectic spot that combines art, music, and nightlife into one unforgettable experience. This venue celebrates creativity with colorful murals, light projections, and interactive art installations. On **Art Pop Thursdays**, the club hosts themed nights featuring live performers and art-inspired DJ sets.

I found myself mesmerized by their curated mix of visuals and beats, which created an almost dreamlike atmosphere. Pair this with their **Leonardo's Gin Fizz**, and you've got yourself a masterpiece of a night.

Club: Luci della Città

- **Address:** Via Giovanni di Pietro, 19, Assisi, Italy
- **Contact:** +39 075 819222

- **Website:** www.lucidellacitta.com
- **Entry Fee:** €15, includes one drink
- **Theme Nights:** Live Band Fridays
- **Opening Hours:** 9:00 PM - 2:00 AM
- **Age Restrictions:** 18+

Luci della Città (City Lights) offers a laid-back yet vibrant nightlife experience. Known for its live music performances, the club frequently features talented local bands and emerging artists. I visited on a **Live Band Friday**, and the energy was infectious—think singalongs, dancing, and cheers from an enthusiastic crowd.

The decor is simple yet cozy, with warm lighting that makes you feel at home. I highly recommend their **Classic Negroni**, which pairs beautifully with the music-filled atmosphere.

Club: Energia Assisi

- **Address:** Strada Mattonata, 88, Assisi, Italy
- **Contact:** +39 075 815678
- **Website:** www.energiaassisi.com
- **Entry Fee:** €18
- **Theme Nights:** High Voltage Saturdays
- **Opening Hours:** 10:00 PM - 4:00 AM
- **Age Restrictions:** 18+

As the name suggests, **Energia Assisi** is all about high-energy vibes. This is the go-to spot for party-goers who want to dance until dawn. The club's futuristic design, with LED-lit walls and pulsating laser lights, sets the tone for a night of non-stop fun.

On **High Voltage Saturdays**, top-notch DJs keep the dance floor packed with a mix of house, techno, and pop tracks. The crowd here is young and lively, making it the perfect spot for those who thrive in a high-octane environment. Don't miss their **Electric Blue Lagoon**, a drink that glows as brightly as the dance floor.

Club: Vibe Social Club

- **Address:** Via Fontebella, 50, Assisi, Italy
- **Contact:** +39 075 812345
- **Website:** www.vibesocialclub.com
- **Entry Fee:** €10
- **Theme Nights:** Open Mic Tuesdays, Acoustic Sundays
- **Opening Hours:** 8:00 PM - 1:00 AM
- **Age Restrictions:** 18+

Vibe Social Club is perfect for those seeking a more intimate and artistic nightlife experience. This hybrid lounge and nightclub caters to creatives and music lovers alike. Their **Open Mic Tuesdays** attract a mix of poets, comedians, and musicians, creating a warm and inclusive vibe.

I visited on an **Acoustic Sunday**, and it felt like I was attending a private concert. The talented performers and laid-back ambiance were a refreshing change from the typical nightclub scene. Pair your evening with their **Honey Lavender Whiskey Sour**, and you're in for a delightful night.

CHAPTER 4: TRAVEL ITINERARIES

Outdoor Adventure Itinerary in Assisi: A Personal Journey

When planning an outdoor adventure in Assisi, I'll admit, my mind initially leaped to its iconic basilicas and art-filled interiors. But the moment I stepped foot into this tranquil Umbrian haven, I realized its offerings extend far beyond its spiritual allure. Assisi is a treasure trove of natural beauty, and its hills, valleys, and quaint countryside make it perfect for outdoor exploration. Here's a full-day itinerary that will let you experience Assisi like an adventurer while soaking in its serene beauty and historical charm.

Morning: Sunrise Trek to Eremo delle Carceri

Start Time: 7:00 AM
There's something magical about mornings in Assisi—the crisp air, the gentle hum of nature waking up, and the warm hues of sunlight spilling over the hills. Begin your adventure with a sunrise trek to **Eremo delle Carceri**, a hermitage nestled in the lush Monte Subasio hills, about 4 km from the town center.

The trail to the hermitage isn't overly strenuous, but it's steep enough to give you a good workout. Walking amidst the towering oak and holm trees, I remember feeling a sense of calm, as if the forest itself were embracing me. Along the way, you might spot locals jogging or a family of wild boars in the undergrowth—reminders of the harmony between man and nature in this region.

The hermitage, where St. Francis retreated for prayer, exudes tranquility. The stone pathways, moss-covered walls, and panoramic views from the site are awe-inspiring. After exploring the hermitage, pause for a moment to take in the view of the Umbrian valley below. Trust me, this moment alone is worth the early start.

Mid-Morning: Nature Walk in Bosco di San Francesco

Start Time: 10:00 AM
Descending back toward Assisi, head straight to the **Bosco di San Francesco**. This enchanting forest is managed by the FAI (Fondo Ambiente Italiano) and is designed as a journey through art, history, and nature.

The walking trail here is about 4 km long and meanders through olive groves, woods, and open meadows. It's not a challenging hike, but the sheer variety of scenery keeps it exciting. I particularly loved the "Third Paradise" installation by Michelangelo Pistoletto—a subtle merging of nature and art in the form of an enormous field sculpture.

Pack some snacks or grab a light sandwich from a local café before entering the forest. There's a quaint picnic area near the end of the trail, where you can sit and enjoy your meal, listening to birdsong and the faint rustle of leaves in the breeze.

Lunch: A Rustic Meal in the Countryside

Start Time: 12:30 PM
After a morning of exploring, you'll have worked up quite an appetite. Drive or cycle to a nearby agriturismo (a farm stay that often offers meals). I chose **Agriturismo Le Mandrie di San Paolo**, about 15 minutes from the Bosco.

The setting is straight out of a dream: rolling hills covered in olive trees and a terrace offering panoramic views of the valley below. Here, I indulged in a hearty plate of strangozzi al tartufo (a local pasta with truffle), paired with a glass of Umbrian wine. The ingredients are farm-to-table, and the flavors are as authentic as they come. Don't rush this experience; it's a chance to soak in the slower pace of life that defines this region.

Early Afternoon: Cycling the Via degli Ulivi

Start Time: 2:30 PM
Refueled and refreshed, it's time to hop on a bike and tackle the **Via degli Ulivi**, or the "Path of the Olive Trees." This cycling route takes you through some of the most scenic parts of the Umbrian countryside, with Assisi as your anchor point.

The path weaves through olive groves, ancient stone villages, and vineyards. It's a fairly easy route, with gentle slopes that even beginners can manage. One stop I'd highly recommend is the town of Spello, just a short detour away. Known for its flower-adorned streets and charming piazzas, Spello is a lovely place to take a break and grab a gelato before continuing your ride.

Late Afternoon: Paragliding Over Monte Subasio

Start Time: 4:30 PM
For thrill-seekers, the highlight of an outdoor adventure in Assisi is undoubtedly paragliding over **Monte Subasio**. As someone who's always been a little nervous about heights, I was hesitant to try it, but the experience turned out to be one of the most exhilarating moments of my life.

From the take-off point near the summit, you'll get a bird's-eye view of Assisi, its surrounding villages, and the expansive Umbrian valley. Floating through the air, with the wind in your face and the world stretched out below you, is nothing short of magical. The instructors are highly experienced, and tandem flights make it accessible even for beginners.

If paragliding isn't your thing, consider hiking a portion of the Monte Subasio ridge instead. The trails are well-marked and offer equally stunning views, albeit from a steadier footing.

Evening: Sunset at Rocca Maggiore

Start Time: 6:30 PM
As the day winds down, make your way to **Rocca Maggiore**, the medieval fortress perched above Assisi. The hike up to the fortress is steep but short, and the reward at the top is priceless: an unobstructed view of the sun setting over the valley.

Watching the golden light bathe Assisi's rooftops, the olive groves, and the rolling hills in the distance, I felt a profound sense of peace. It's a moment that stays with you—a reminder of the beauty that comes from simply being present in nature.

Dinner: Al Fresco Dining in Assisi

Start Time: 8:00 PM
Wrap up your day with dinner at an outdoor trattoria in Assisi's town center. I recommend **Trattoria Pallotta**, located near Piazza del Comune. The outdoor seating lets you dine under the stars, with the soft glow of the city's lights adding to the ambiance.

Order the roasted lamb or the Umbrian lentil soup, both of which are local specialties. Pair it with another glass of Sagrantino wine, and let the day's adventures sink in. If you're lucky, you might even catch a street musician playing softly nearby, completing the perfect ending to your outdoor adventure.

A Romantic Itinerary in Assisi

Assisi, nestled in the heart of Umbria, is more than just a quaint Italian town; it's a place that stirs the soul and heightens emotions. With its cobblestone streets, ancient churches, and sweeping views of the Umbrian countryside, Assisi is perfect for couples seeking a romantic escape. Let me take you on a journey through a dreamy two-day itinerary, infused with personal touches and highlights that will make your visit unforgettable.

Day 1: Exploring the Charms of Assisi

Morning: Sunrise Over the Basilica of St. Francis

Start your romantic adventure early with a sunrise view at the Basilica of St. Francis of Assisi. There's something magical about watching the first rays of sunlight bathe the sprawling valley below in golden hues. The basilica itself is breathtaking, with its magnificent frescoes by Giotto and Cimabue. Walking hand-in-hand through the Lower and Upper Basilicas, the silence and reverence make you feel deeply connected—not just to the history but also to each other.

Take your time here. After all, the pace of Assisi encourages you to slow down and savor every moment. You can sit on one of the nearby benches and share a quiet moment as the world wakes up around you.

Late Morning: Strolling Through Medieval Streets

From the basilica, wander toward Piazza del Comune, Assisi's central square. The streets are straight out of a fairytale—lined with stone houses, tiny artisan shops, and flower-filled balconies. One of my favorite things to do was duck into the little boutiques selling handmade ceramics and olive wood carvings. These make perfect souvenirs or mementos of your trip.

The square itself is vibrant yet calm, with the Fountain of Minerva and its Roman Temple standing proudly in the center. If you're like me and can't resist people-watching, find a café with outdoor seating and enjoy a cappuccino while soaking in the atmosphere.

Lunch: A Romantic Meal at Osteria Piazzetta dell'Erba

For lunch, indulge in authentic Umbrian cuisine at Osteria Piazzetta dell'Erba, tucked away near the main square. This intimate spot is known for its farm-to-table philosophy and creative take on traditional dishes. I remember ordering the truffle pasta, and it was heavenly. Paired with a glass of local white wine, it felt like the food was as much a love letter to the region as the town itself.

The soft lighting and cozy atmosphere make it an ideal setting to share meaningful conversations and a few laughs. Trust me, this is the kind of meal you'll both remember long after the trip ends.

Afternoon: Visiting the Rocca Maggiore

After lunch, take a leisurely walk to Rocca Maggiore, a medieval fortress perched high above Assisi. The path leading to the fortress winds through lush greenery, and the views at the top are worth every step. From up here, you can see the entire valley spread out before you—a patchwork of olive groves, vineyards, and villages.

Exploring the fortress together feels like stepping into a chapter of history. There's a thrill in imagining knights and royals who once roamed these walls. And if you're lucky, you might catch the golden hour here, with the warm sunlight casting a romantic glow over the landscape.

Evening: Sunset Dinner at Ristorante Metastasio

End your day with a romantic dinner at Ristorante Metastasio, known for its panoramic terrace overlooking the Umbrian countryside. As the sun sets, the sky turns shades of pink and orange, creating the perfect backdrop for a memorable evening.

The menu is a love letter to Umbria, featuring dishes like wild boar stew and saffron risotto. Sharing a bottle of Sagrantino wine, a regional specialty, is a must. I can still picture the candlelit table, the laughter shared, and the feeling of complete contentment as the evening unfolded.

Day 2: Immersing in Assisi's Serenity

Morning: Quiet Moments at the Hermitage of the Carceri

Start your second day with a visit to the Eremo delle Carceri, a hermitage nestled in the forests of Monte Subasio. This sacred retreat is a short drive from Assisi, and the journey itself, winding through cypress-lined roads, feels like a romantic escape.

The hermitage is where St. Francis and his followers came for solitude and prayer. Walking through its tranquil pathways, with the sound of birds and the rustle of leaves as your soundtrack, is profoundly calming. It's a place that inspires quiet reflection, and being there with your partner feels incredibly intimate.

Late Morning: Exploring Santa Maria degli Angeli

Return to Assisi and visit the Basilica of Santa Maria degli Angeli, located at the foot of the hill. This grand church houses the Porziuncola, a tiny chapel where St. Francis first established his order. The contrast between the small, humble chapel and the grand basilica that envelops it is striking.

Outside the basilica, there's a rose garden said to have grown miraculously without thorns. Take a walk here—it's a quiet, romantic spot perfect for holding hands and sharing a peaceful moment.

Lunch: A Farm-to-Table Experience at Agriturismo Il Castello

For lunch, head to Agriturismo Il Castello, a charming farmhouse just outside Assisi. This family-run establishment serves fresh, seasonal dishes made with ingredients straight from their farm. Imagine dining on a sunny terrace with panoramic views, sharing plates of bruschetta, roasted meats, and the best tiramisu I've ever tasted.

The rustic charm and genuine hospitality here make it feel like you've stumbled upon a hidden gem. It's one of those meals where the setting and the food combine to create pure magic.

Afternoon: Art and Inspiration at San Damiano

After lunch, visit the Church of San Damiano, a peaceful sanctuary just a short distance from the town center. This is where St. Francis is said to have received his divine calling, and it's also closely linked to St. Clare, who founded her order here.

The simplicity of the church and its surrounding gardens is incredibly moving. Sitting on a bench under the olive trees, with the Umbrian hills stretching out before you, is the perfect moment to pause and soak in the beauty of the day.

Evening: A Romantic Stroll and Farewell Dinner

As your time in Assisi draws to a close, take a leisurely evening stroll through the town's softly lit streets. There's something magical about Assisi at night—the quiet alleys, the glow of lanterns, and the occasional strains of music from a nearby piazza.

For your farewell dinner, I recommend Trattoria Pallotta, located near the Piazza del Comune. This cozy, family-run restaurant serves traditional dishes with a modern twist. Their gnocchi with truffle sauce is divine, and the dessert menu is a must-try—especially the panna cotta.

Toast to your unforgettable trip with a glass of Prosecco, and let the evening linger as long as you like. There's no rush in Assisi;

the town seems to bend time to its will, allowing you to savor every moment.

Coastal Itinerary in Assisi: A Journey Through Charm and Serenity

When I first thought of Assisi, the vision of a coastal adventure didn't immediately come to mind. After all, this historic hilltop town in Umbria is renowned for its religious significance, medieval architecture, and connection to St. Francis. But as I delved deeper into the surrounding regions and planned an extended stay, I discovered how Assisi can serve as a gateway to coastal-like experiences in nearby areas, blending tranquil waters, scenic drives, and hidden gems.

If you're like me—someone who loves to mix a touch of history with breezy waterside moments—then this itinerary is for you. Let's dive into a journey where Assisi becomes your central hub to explore the soul-soothing coasts of nearby lakes and coastal-style towns.

Day 1: Arrival in Assisi – Immerse Yourself in Its Essence

Morning:
There's nothing quite like the first sight of Assisi. As you approach, the town seems to rise like a medieval dream out of the rolling Umbrian hills. Check into your accommodation—something quaint, like **Nun Assisi Relais & Spa Museum**, which perfectly blends modern luxury with the historical charm of the area.

Once settled, take a leisurely walk to **Basilica di San Francesco d'Assisi**. The serenity of this sacred space, combined with its breathtaking frescoes by Giotto, sets the tone for the reflective and awe-filled journey ahead.

Afternoon:
Stop for lunch at **Osteria Piazzetta dell'Erba**, a cozy eatery with dishes that celebrate Umbrian flavors. The truffle pasta here is divine, and the wines pair beautifully with the meal.

Evening:
Spend the evening strolling along the cobblestone streets of Assisi. Watch the sunset from **Rocca Maggiore**, a hilltop fortress with panoramic views that stretch far enough to hint at the adventures awaiting outside the town.

Day 2: Assisi to Lake Trasimeno – A Taste of Coastal Tranquility

Morning:
Start your day early with a scenic 45-minute drive to **Lake Trasimeno**, Italy's fourth-largest lake and often referred to as "the sea of Umbria." As you near the lake, the sparkling waters and lush greenery immediately transport you to a coastal-like setting.

Head to the town of **Passignano sul Trasimeno**, a charming lakeside village. Begin with a cappuccino and pastry at **Bar Cristallo**, sitting by the lake as the gentle waves lap against the shore.

Midday:
For a truly immersive experience, take a ferry to **Isola Maggiore**, a small island in the lake. This is where I found myself losing track

of time, wandering through quiet streets lined with lace shops (a local specialty) and enjoying the peaceful atmosphere.

Lunch Recommendation: Ristorante L'Isola Verde on the island serves freshly caught fish from the lake. Their grilled perch with a side of roasted vegetables is an absolute must-try.

Afternoon Adventure:
After returning to the mainland, rent a bike and follow one of the cycling trails that hug the lake's shoreline. The trails are well-marked and offer stunning views, especially if you time your ride to coincide with the golden hour.

Evening:
Wrap up the day with a leisurely dinner at **Il Molo**, a restaurant right on the water. Their seafood risotto, combined with a local Umbrian white wine, is the perfect way to end your first coastal-inspired day.

Day 3: Coastal Charm in Orbetello – The Tuscan Lagoon Experience

Morning:
For a change of scenery, make an early start and drive about two hours west to **Orbetello**, a stunning lagoon town in southern Tuscany. While it's a bit of a journey, the road trip itself is part of the charm, as the Umbrian hills slowly give way to coastal landscapes.

Once you arrive, you'll notice how Orbetello seems to float on water, thanks to its unique location on a thin strip of land surrounded by lagoons.

Midday:
Head to **Spiaggia della Feniglia**, a pristine beach that stretches for miles. Whether you want to swim, sunbathe, or take a long walk along the shore, this beach has something for everyone. The pine forest bordering the beach adds a layer of natural beauty and shade.

Lunch Spot: For lunch, try **I Pescatori di Orbetello**, a local favorite serving up freshly caught seafood. Their spaghetti alle vongole (clams) was hands-down the best I've ever had.

Afternoon Stroll:
Explore the town itself in the afternoon. The pedestrian-friendly streets, historic gates, and lively piazzas make Orbetello a joy to wander through. Don't miss the **Duomo di Santa Maria Assunta**, a beautiful cathedral with a blend of Gothic and Renaissance elements.

Evening:
Before heading back to Assisi, enjoy an early dinner at **La Rosa dei Venti**, located near the lagoon. The sunset views over the water, paired with their seafood specialties, are unforgettable.

Day 4: Spello and Bevagna – Hidden Gems Near Assisi

Morning:
Today, stay closer to Assisi and explore the nearby towns of **Spello** and **Bevagna**. While these towns aren't coastal, they exude a tranquil charm that complements the coastal vibes of your previous days.

Begin in Spello, just a 15-minute drive from Assisi. Known for its flower-filled streets and ancient Roman mosaics, Spello is perfect for a relaxed morning stroll. Stop by **Bar Bonci** for a coffee and a slice of freshly baked ciambella.

Midday:
Drive another 20 minutes to **Bevagna**, a medieval town famous for its artisan workshops and slow pace of life. Visit the **Piazza Silvestri**, where you can admire the beautiful Romanesque churches and perhaps join a local artisan for a quick workshop.

Lunch Recommendation: Dine at **Antiche Sere**, a family-run trattoria known for its hearty Umbrian dishes. Their handmade strangozzi pasta with wild boar ragu is the definition of comfort food.

Afternoon and Evening:
Return to Assisi and spend your evening indulging in a relaxing spa session at your hotel. After days of exploring, a massage or soak in a thermal bath feels heavenly.

Day 5: Departure – A Morning of Reflection

Before leaving Assisi, spend your last morning soaking in the tranquility of this sacred town. Head to **Eremo delle Carceri**, a hermitage nestled in the forested slopes of Mount Subasio. The peaceful atmosphere here offers a perfect moment of reflection, allowing you to gather your thoughts and cherish the memories made during your coastal-inspired adventure.

Budget-friendly itinerary in Assisi

Assisi, a charming hill town in Italy's Umbria region, is a place that holds an almost ethereal beauty. Known for its connection to St. Francis, the patron saint of animals and the environment, Assisi has this serene vibe that makes you feel as if you've stepped into a time capsule. While it might seem like a destination for luxury retreats, I discovered it's entirely possible to explore this gem on a budget. Here's how I did it.

The first step in saving money is how you arrive. If you're coming from Rome or Florence, take the regional train instead of the high-speed one. It's slower, but for under €15, you can soak in scenic countryside views that make the extra travel time worth it. The train drops you off at the Santa Maria degli Angeli station, a short bus ride or a 30-minute uphill walk to Assisi. I opted for the bus (just €1.50 if you buy the ticket beforehand at a tabacchi shop).

For budget travelers, Assisi offers plenty of choices. Hostels and budget-friendly guesthouses are scattered throughout the town. I stayed at **Ostello della Pace**, which was a steal at around €25 a night for a dorm bed. It's cozy, with a communal kitchen where I met fellow travelers over shared meals. If you're traveling with someone, check out small family-run B&Bs; some offer double rooms for as low as €50 a night, including breakfast.

Day 1: Exploring Assisi's Historic Core

Morning
Start your day early because the magic of Assisi is best felt in the quiet mornings. The first stop? The **Basilica of St. Francis**, of course. Entry is free, and trust me, this UNESCO World Heritage Site is breathtaking. The basilica is actually two churches, one stacked on top of the other, with frescoes by Giotto that are stunning. I spent nearly two hours marveling at the artwork and the peaceful aura of the place.

Tip: Arrive before 9 AM to avoid the crowds and enjoy a more meditative experience.

Afternoon
Lunch doesn't have to break the bank. I grabbed a porchetta sandwich (succulent roasted pork) from a small deli near the Piazza del Comune for just €5. There's no shortage of little cafes and bakeries offering delicious paninis or slices of torta al testo (Umbrian flatbread filled with cheese or prosciutto). Pair it with a €2 espresso, and you're set.

After lunch, explore the **Piazza del Comune**, the town's main square. The **Temple of Minerva**, which has been turned into a church, is a must-see. It's free to enter, and its Roman columns give you a fascinating glimpse of Assisi's ancient history.

From there, wander through the cobblestone streets, stopping by small artisan shops. Even if you're not buying anything, it's delightful to watch artisans at work, crafting ceramics and textiles that feel like they belong in another era.

Evening
For dinner, head to a **trattoria** like Trattoria Pallotta. Their fixed menu (around €15) includes a primo (pasta), secondo (meat or vegetarian dish), and dessert. It's a cozy spot with authentic Umbrian flavors that won't dent your budget.

Day 2: Embracing Nature and More Spiritual Sites

Morning
I started the day with a hike to **Eremo delle Carceri**, a hermitage nestled in the woods on Monte Subasio, just outside Assisi. If you love walking, you can take the scenic route uphill for free. It's about 4 km, and the views along the way are rewarding.

Alternatively, the local bus costs about €2. The hermitage itself is free to enter, and it's one of the most peaceful spots I've ever visited. You'll find yourself surrounded by nature, with small caves and chapels where monks once meditated.

Afternoon
On the way back, stop by the **San Damiano Church**, another free site that's often overlooked but incredibly meaningful. This is where St. Francis wrote the "Canticle of the Creatures," and the simplicity of the place is moving.

For lunch, I visited a small trattoria outside the main tourist area. Many places offer **"menu del giorno"** (daily specials) for around €10-12, which typically includes a pasta dish and a glass of house wine. The homemade tagliatelle with wild boar ragu I had was divine.

Evening
In the evening, walk along Assisi's city walls for panoramic views of the valley below. Watching the sunset from **Rocca Maggiore**, the medieval fortress at the top of the hill, is a memory that stays with you. Entry is around €6, but if you're traveling off-season or late in the day, you might find it open for free.

Day 3: Discovering Nearby Gems

Morning
On my last day, I ventured down to **Santa Maria degli Angeli**, where the magnificent Basilica of the same name is located. This church houses the Porziuncola, the tiny chapel where St. Francis founded the Franciscan Order. It's free to enter, and its grandeur is a sharp contrast to the humble chapel inside.

Afternoon
For a change of scenery, consider a quick trip to the nearby town of Spello. A round-trip train ticket costs under €5, and Spello is like a smaller, quieter version of Assisi. Its streets are lined with flowers, and its frescoes, particularly in the **Santa Maria Maggiore Church**, are stunning (entry is just €2). I grabbed a picnic lunch—fresh bread, cheese, and olives from a local market—for under €8 and enjoyed it while overlooking the rolling Umbrian hills.

Evening
Back in Assisi, I treated myself to a budget-friendly splurge: a gelato from **Bar Bibiano**, one of the best gelaterias in town. For €3, you get a generous scoop of creamy, locally inspired flavors like pistachio or fig. Walking the quiet, softly lit streets of Assisi with gelato in hand felt like the perfect way to end my trip.

Budget-Friendly Tips for Assisi

1. **Walking is free and rewarding**: Assisi is small and best explored on foot. You'll save on transportation and discover hidden alleys and views.
2. **Visit during shoulder seasons**: April-May and September-October see fewer tourists, and accommodation prices drop significantly.
3. **Pack snacks and water**: Groceries in Assisi are reasonably priced. I bought fruits, nuts, and water from a small shop for under €5, which kept me fueled during long walks.
4. **Free attractions abound**: Many churches, viewpoints, and historic sites in Assisi don't charge entry, allowing you to immerse yourself in its rich culture without spending a dime.

Historical Itinerary in Assisi

When I first stepped foot into Assisi, I was struck by its palpable sense of history. The city seemed to whisper tales of centuries gone by, its cobblestone streets and ancient stone buildings radiating a timeless charm. Nestled on the slopes of Mount Subasio in the Umbria region of Italy, Assisi is a treasure trove for history lovers. Let me take you on a journey through this enchanting city, following an itinerary that lets you soak in its historical depth while savoring its serene atmosphere.

Morning: Start at the Basilica of San Francesco

Your day begins with the heart of Assisi's history: the **Basilica of San Francesco**. As you approach the basilica, its imposing yet graceful façade is a sight to behold. This UNESCO World Heritage Site is not just a church; it's a living monument to Saint Francis of Assisi, the patron saint of animals and ecology.

When I entered, I was overwhelmed by the frescoes adorning the walls and ceilings. Created by legendary artists such as Giotto and Cimabue, these frescoes vividly narrate the life of Saint Francis. The Lower Basilica feels solemn and intimate, while the Upper Basilica opens up with a brighter, more celestial atmosphere. I remember spending an hour simply sitting on one of the pews, marveling at the artwork and feeling the peace that enveloped the space.

Take your time to explore the adjoining monastery, the **Sacred Convent**, which houses an impressive library and museum. It's fascinating to see artifacts that have survived centuries, each carrying a fragment of Assisi's story.

Mid-Morning: Stroll Through Piazza del Comune

From the basilica, wander uphill towards **Piazza del Comune**, the main square. This piazza is the beating heart of Assisi, lined with historic buildings and bustling with life. I recommend grabbing a quick espresso at one of the cafés here – sipping coffee while watching the world go by is one of my favorite ways to soak in the atmosphere.

The square itself is steeped in history. You'll find the **Temple of Minerva**, a Roman temple that dates back to the 1st century BC. Its transformation into a Christian church, the **Santa Maria sopra Minerva**, is a testament to Assisi's layered history. Standing before its six Corinthian columns, I couldn't help but marvel at how this ancient structure has withstood the test of time.

Late Morning: Climb to Rocca Maggiore

A visit to Assisi wouldn't be complete without a trek up to the **Rocca Maggiore**, the medieval fortress that crowns the town. The walk is steep but rewarding, offering panoramic views of the Umbrian countryside. I remember pausing several times along the way, not just to catch my breath, but to admire the rolling hills dotted with olive groves and vineyards.

The fortress itself is a marvel of medieval architecture. Built in the 12th century, it served as a defensive stronghold and a symbol of power. As I wandered through its stone corridors and climbed its towers, I felt transported back to a time when knights and nobles roamed these halls. Don't miss the topmost tower – the views are absolutely breathtaking, and it's the perfect spot for photos.

Lunch: A Taste of Umbrian History

By now, you'll have worked up an appetite, and Assisi's culinary scene doesn't disappoint. Head to a local trattoria, such as **Trattoria Pallotta**, located near Piazza del Comune. I remember trying their **umbricelli pasta**, a thick, hand-rolled pasta typical of the region, served with a rich truffle sauce. Pair it with a glass of local Sagrantino wine, and you'll feel as though you're dining like a medieval noble.

Afternoon: Explore the Basilica of Santa Chiara

After lunch, make your way to the **Basilica of Santa Chiara**. Dedicated to Saint Clare, a close companion of Saint Francis and the founder of the Order of Poor Clares, this church is both beautiful and spiritually moving. Its pale pink façade, built from local Subasio stone, glows softly in the afternoon light.

Inside, you'll find relics of Saint Clare and a simple yet striking crucifix that is said to have spoken to Saint Francis, urging him to "rebuild my church." I remember standing before it, imagining the moment that sparked a movement that changed the course of history.

Late Afternoon: The Hermitage of the Carceri

If you're up for a short drive or a hike, head to the **Hermitage of the Carceri**, located in a quiet, wooded area on Mount Subasio. This hermitage was a retreat for Saint Francis and his followers, where they sought solitude and communion with nature.

Walking through the forested trails leading to the hermitage, I felt an incredible sense of peace. The tiny stone chapels and caves seem almost untouched by time, and the air is filled with the scent of pine and wildflowers. It's easy to see why Saint Francis felt so connected to this place.

Evening: Sunset at San Damiano

As the day winds down, there's no better place to watch the sunset than **San Damiano**, a small church and monastery on the outskirts of Assisi. This was where Saint Francis received his calling to rebuild the church and where Saint Clare spent much of her life.

The view from San Damiano is simply magical. As the sun sets, the Umbrian countryside is bathed in a golden glow, and the tranquility of the moment is unforgettable. I remember sitting on a stone bench outside the church, feeling a deep connection to the history and spirituality of the place.

Dinner: An Evening to Remember

End your day with dinner at **La Locanda del Cardinale**, an elegant restaurant housed in a historic building with Roman ruins visible beneath the glass floor. The ambiance is unmatched, and the food is a perfect blend of traditional Umbrian flavors and modern culinary artistry. I recommend the roasted lamb or the wild boar stew – both are divine.

Optional: Nighttime Stroll

Before retiring for the night, take a leisurely stroll through Assisi's streets. The city takes on a magical quality after dark, with its stone buildings softly lit and the sounds of the day replaced by a peaceful hush. I found myself wandering aimlessly, letting the quiet beauty of Assisi wash over me.

A Family-Friendly Itinerary in Assisi: A Journey of Wonder and Togetherness

If there's one destination in Italy that feels like a magical retreat for families, it's Assisi. Nestled in the heart of Umbria, this quaint hilltop town offers a mix of history, spirituality, nature, and charm that captivates visitors of all ages. From my own experience wandering Assisi's cobblestone streets with my family, I can assure you that this itinerary balances adventure, relaxation, and cultural immersion—perfect for creating lifelong memories.

Day 1: Arrival and First Impressions of Assisi

Morning: Arrive in Assisi and Settle In

Arriving in Assisi feels like stepping into a storybook. After checking into a cozy family-friendly hotel (I recommend **Hotel Ideale** with its stunning terrace views), take a moment to soak in the serene atmosphere. The town's terracotta rooftops and olive groves stretching out to the horizon provide the perfect backdrop for your adventure.

Afternoon: Explore the Basilica of St. Francis

A visit to the **Basilica of St. Francis** is a must. While you might think a religious site could bore the little ones, the frescoes by Giotto tell stories that even kids can appreciate. We played a game of "spot the animals" in the artwork, which kept everyone engaged. Remember to whisper, as this is a sacred space.

Pro tip: Visit the lower basilica first, as it's less crowded. The peaceful courtyard nearby is perfect for a quick snack break—pack some local pastries or fruits from a market.

Evening: Piazza del Comune and Dinner

The **Piazza del Comune** comes alive in the evening, making it the ideal spot for families. Kids can run around safely while parents relax at a café. We loved trying the local pizza at **Ristorante La Fortezza**, where the friendly staff made us feel at home.

Day 2: Immersing in Assisi's Charm and Nature

Morning: Walk the Rocca Maggiore

After a hearty breakfast, head to the **Rocca Maggiore**, a medieval fortress with panoramic views. While the steep walk might seem daunting, it's manageable with frequent breaks. For kids, the promise of exploring a real castle with towers and hidden corners is irresistible. Bring a pair of binoculars for some birdwatching from the top!

Midday: Picnic in Parco del Monte Subasio

Pack a picnic and head to **Parco del Monte Subasio**, just outside the town. The park is a lush green haven where families can unwind. My kids loved chasing butterflies while we lounged under the shade of a tree, enjoying sandwiches and fresh local cheese.

Afternoon: Visit the Porziuncola in Santa Maria degli Angeli

The **Porziuncola**, a tiny chapel within the grand **Basilica of Santa Maria degli Angeli**, is a hidden gem. Its significance and simplicity resonated even with the kids, especially after hearing how St. Francis himself prayed there. The nearby rose garden is lovely for a quick stroll.

Evening: Cooking Class for the Whole Family

For dinner, why not learn to make your own Italian meal? Many local cooking schools in Assisi, like **Sapori Umbri**, offer family-friendly classes. Rolling out pasta dough together and learning to make tiramisu was a highlight of our trip. Plus, eating what you've made adds a special flavor to the experience.

Day 3: Art, Crafts, and Farewell

Morning: Explore Artisan Workshops

Assisi is known for its traditional crafts, and visiting an artisan workshop is a treat. We stopped by **Studio Moretti Caselli**, a stained-glass workshop, where the kids were fascinated by the intricate designs. Some workshops even allow hands-on activities, like creating small mosaics.

Midday: Lunch at Trattoria Pallotta

Enjoy a leisurely lunch at **Trattoria Pallotta**, a cozy spot near Piazza del Comune. They serve classic Umbrian dishes with a modern twist, and the kids' menu is surprisingly diverse. The staff even gave our little ones crayons and paper to keep them entertained.

Afternoon: Visit Eremo delle Carceri

The **Eremo delle Carceri**, a hermitage tucked away in the woods of Mount Subasio, is a peaceful escape. The forest trails leading to the hermitage are manageable for families, and the site itself is both serene and thought-provoking. It's a great place to introduce children to the concepts of simplicity and connection with nature.

Evening: Gelato and Farewell Walk

What's a trip to Italy without gelato? End your journey with scoops of creamy gelato from **Bar Bibiano**, then take a slow walk along Assisi's lit-up streets. Watching the sunset from one of the town's viewpoints, such as **Piazza San Rufino**, is the perfect way to say goodbye.

Tips for a Smooth Family Trip to Assisi

1. **Timing Is Key:** Assisi is busiest during the middle of the day. Plan visits to popular sites early in the morning or late in the afternoon to avoid crowds.
2. **Stay Central:** Choose accommodation within walking distance of major attractions to minimize travel time and keep the kids' energy levels high.
3. **Pack Light Snacks:** While Assisi has plenty of dining options, having snacks on hand can save the day during unexpected delays.
4. **Interactive Games:** Keep kids engaged by turning historical sites into treasure hunts or storytelling opportunities.

5. **Flexibility Matters:** Allow extra time for wandering and impromptu breaks. Assisi's charm often lies in the unplanned moments.

Why Assisi Works for Families

Assisi's small size, welcoming locals, and blend of history and nature make it an ideal destination for families. It's a place where children can run freely, parents can relax, and everyone can reconnect. From medieval castles to serene parks and the joy of learning about St. Francis, this itinerary offers something for every member of the family.

As you plan your journey, remember that Assisi isn't just a place—it's an experience that unfolds gently, leaving you with memories to cherish long after you've left its cobblestone streets.

CHAPTER 5: CULTURAL EXPERIENCES

Festivals in Assisi: A Journey Through Tradition, Celebration, and Spirit

Assisi is a town that lives and breathes its heritage, and this comes to life in its vibrant festivals. Whether you're wandering through the cobbled streets, soaking in the medieval architecture, or enjoying the breathtaking views of the Umbrian countryside, the festivals of Assisi add another layer of magic to this already enchanting place. Let me take you on a journey through a few of these festivals that I've had the privilege to experience, sharing not only the highlights but also some tips to help you make the most of your visit.

Festival: Calendimaggio

- **Location**: Historic center of Assisi
- **Date**: First Thursday, Friday, and Saturday in May
- **Activities**: Medieval reenactments, music, parades, and flag-throwing competitions
- **Tips for Visitors**: Arrive early to secure a good viewing spot; wear comfortable shoes as you'll walk on cobbled streets.

Ah, the Calendimaggio! The festival takes you straight back to the Middle Ages, with Assisi's streets brimming with vibrant costumes, medieval music, and the unmistakable energy of a town divided into two rival factions: the Parte de Sopra (Upper Part) and Parte de Sotto (Lower Part). The competition between these factions is fierce, but it's all in good fun.

When I visited, the opening procession was nothing short of mesmerizing. The participants, clad in elaborate medieval attire, moved through the streets with a sense of purpose, transporting everyone to a time when Assisi's walls were lined with knights and maidens. The evening performances were my favorite. Watching the flag-throwers coordinate their daring routines under the glow of torchlight is a memory I'll never forget.

Pro Tip: Book your accommodations in Assisi well in advance if you plan to attend. The town fills up quickly, and having a central base means you can experience the festival to its fullest without worrying about long commutes.

Festival: Feast of St. Francis

- **Location**: Basilica of St. Francis and town center
- **Date**: October 4 (with events leading up to the day)
- **Activities**: Religious processions, Mass, and cultural performances
- **Tips for Visitors**: Respect the solemn nature of this event; dress modestly, especially when entering churches.

This festival is a deeply spiritual occasion, celebrating Assisi's most famous son, St. Francis. As a traveler who values meaningful experiences, I found this event profoundly moving. The town takes on a reverent yet celebratory air as pilgrims from all over the world gather to honor the patron saint of Italy.

The highlight of my visit was the candlelit procession leading up to the Basilica of St. Francis. The quiet hum of hymns filled the night air as the procession wove through Assisi's streets. On the day of the feast, I attended a solemn Mass at the basilica, which was packed with locals and visitors alike. Despite the crowd, there was a sense of intimacy in the shared reverence.

Pro Tip: Arrive at the basilica early for major events like the procession and Mass. If you can, plan your visit to include some of the lesser-known churches, like the Hermitage of the Carceri, for a quieter reflection on St. Francis's life.

Festival: Palio di San Rufino

- **Location**: Piazza San Rufino and surrounding streets
- **Date**: Last weekend in August
- **Activities**: Archery competition, medieval games, parades, and music
- **Tips for Visitors**: Check the schedule for the archery finals—they're the highlight of the festival.

The Palio di San Rufino is all about archery and community spirit. The festival celebrates Assisi's patron saint, St. Rufino, with a unique competition where archers from different neighborhoods face off to win the coveted Palio (banner). As someone who loves a mix of tradition and friendly rivalry, this festival hit all the right notes.

I arrived just in time to catch the opening parade. The participants marched in medieval costumes, carrying flags representing their neighborhoods. The real excitement, though, was the archery competition. Watching the archers hit their marks with precision while the crowd cheered them on was thrilling. Later in the evening, I joined locals at the piazza for traditional Umbrian dishes and live music—a perfect way to wind down after a day of festivities.

Pro Tip: Don't miss the chance to try local specialties sold during the festival. The porchetta sandwiches and wild boar stew were my personal favorites.

Festival: Christmas in Assisi

- **Location**: Throughout Assisi, especially Piazza del Comune
- **Date**: December (entire month, with key events around Christmas Day)
- **Activities**: Live nativity scenes, Christmas markets, concerts, and light displays
- **Tips for Visitors**: Bundle up! Assisi can get chilly in December, but the festive atmosphere will keep you warm.

Assisi at Christmas is a dream come true. The town transforms into a winter wonderland, with twinkling lights adorning the medieval streets and a giant nativity scene set up in Piazza del Comune. It was like stepping into a Christmas card.

The live nativity scenes were the standout for me. Locals dressed as Mary, Joseph, shepherds, and the Three Wise Men brought the Christmas story to life with such authenticity that it was hard not to feel the magic of the season. The markets were also a treat, offering everything from handmade ornaments to delicious holiday treats like panettone and torrone.

Pro Tip: If you're visiting with children, check out the workshops where kids can learn to make traditional crafts or bake holiday cookies. It's a fantastic way to immerse them in the festive spirit.

Festival: Festa delle Rose (Feast of the Roses)

- **Location**: Basilica of Santa Maria degli Angeli
- **Date**: End of May or early June

- **Activities**: Religious ceremonies, rose-themed offerings, and processions
- **Tips for Visitors**: Take time to visit the Rose Garden at the basilica—it's stunning during the festival.

This lesser-known festival celebrates St. Clare, one of Assisi's most beloved figures and a close companion of St. Francis. The focus is on roses, symbolizing Clare's purity and devotion. I stumbled upon this festival during a spring visit and was enchanted by its serene beauty.

The highlight for me was the Rose Blessing Ceremony at the Basilica of Santa Maria degli Angeli. The scent of roses filled the air as priests blessed baskets of flowers, which were later distributed to the congregation. It felt like a celebration of both nature and spirituality, perfectly in line with Assisi's character.

Pro Tip: Combine your visit with a tour of the basilica's museum, where you'll find artifacts related to St. Clare and the Franciscan order. It adds depth to the experience.

Insider Tips for Festival-Goers in Assisi

1. **Plan Ahead**: Many festivals in Assisi draw large crowds, so it's wise to plan your accommodations, transportation, and festival schedules in advance.
2. **Blend In**: While tourists are always welcome, showing respect for the local culture by dressing appropriately and participating respectfully will earn you smiles from locals.
3. **Try Local Delights**: Food and drink stalls are a staple at most festivals. Don't miss the chance to savor regional Umbrian specialties—your taste buds will thank you!
4. **Be Prepared to Walk**: Assisi's charm lies in its hilly terrain and winding streets. Comfortable shoes are a must,

especially during festivals when you'll likely be on your feet all day.
5. **Immerse Yourself**: Festivals are a fantastic opportunity to connect with locals. Strike up a conversation, join in the singing or dancing, and let the town's spirit pull you in.

Museums and Galleries in Assisi

When visiting Assisi, it's impossible not to feel the profound intertwining of history, art, and spirituality. The museums and galleries here are like stepping into living storybooks, each telling tales of the city's deep cultural roots. Let me take you on a journey through some of the most unforgettable spots, sharing personal anecdotes and tips as if we were exploring them together.

1. Museo e Foro Romano

- **Address:** Piazza del Comune, 06081 Assisi PG, Italy
- **Contact:** +39 075 8138680
- **Website:** www.museoassisi.it
- **Opening Hours:** 10:00 AM
- **Closing Hours:** 6:00 PM
- **Admission Fee:** €8
- **Special Exhibits:** Rotating displays of Roman artifacts
- **Directions:** Located in the heart of Piazza del Comune, just a short walk from the Basilica of Santa Chiara.

The Roman Forum Museum feels like stepping back in time. I remember descending the stairs and being immediately struck by the ancient stonework—surprisingly well-preserved after centuries. Walking through the underground crypts, you see mosaics, inscriptions, and even remnants of an ancient market.

The staff here are incredibly knowledgeable, and during my visit, a guide pointed out small details I'd have missed on my own, like faint chisel marks from when the stones were first laid. Plan for about 1.5 to 2 hours here, but be sure to linger—it's a serene, almost meditative experience that connects you to the past.

2. Pinacoteca Comunale (Municipal Art Gallery)

- **Address:** Via San Francesco, 12, 06081 Assisi PG, Italy
- **Contact:** +39 075 812179
- **Website:** www.pinacotecacomunaleassisi.it
- **Opening Hours:** 10:00 AM
- **Closing Hours:** 7:00 PM
- **Admission Fee:** €6
- **Special Exhibits:** Frescoes and medieval art
- **Directions:** A few steps down Via San Francesco, near the Basilica of San Francesco.

I discovered the Pinacoteca by accident during my stroll down Via San Francesco. It's a quiet space, but packed with incredible art from the Middle Ages and Renaissance. The highlight for me was a series of frescoes depicting the life of St. Francis.

If you're an art lover, you'll be mesmerized. Even if you're not, the sheer vibrancy of the colors and the intricacy of the storytelling in these pieces will leave an impression. I recommend setting aside at least 1.5 hours, especially if you want to soak in the detailed captions and exhibits.

3. Museo della Memoria (Museum of Memory)

- **Address:** Piazza del Vescovado, 3, 06081 Assisi PG, Italy

- **Contact:** +39 075 813086
- **Website:** www.museodellamemoriaassisi.it
- **Opening Hours:** 9:30 AM
- **Closing Hours:** 5:30 PM
- **Admission Fee:** Free
- **Special Exhibits:** Stories of local heroes during World War II
- **Directions:** Located near the Bishop's Palace, about 10 minutes' walk from the Basilica of St. Francis.

This museum is deeply moving, documenting Assisi's role in sheltering Jewish families during World War II. I was particularly touched by the handwritten letters and photographs that brought the stories to life. There's something incredibly humbling about seeing these pieces of history in the town where it all happened.

It's not a large museum, so you can comfortably spend an hour here, but the emotional impact lingers long after you leave. If you're like me, you'll leave with a newfound appreciation for the resilience and compassion of this small community.

4. Galleria d'Arte Contemporanea (Contemporary Art Gallery)

- **Address:** Via Portica, 7, 06081 Assisi PG, Italy
- **Contact:** +39 075 8190880
- **Website:** www.artemodernaassisi.it
- **Opening Hours:** 10:00 AM
- **Closing Hours:** 8:00 PM
- **Admission Fee:** €5
- **Special Exhibits:** Modern interpretations of Assisi's history and themes of spirituality
- **Directions:** On Via Portica, easily accessible from Piazza del Comune.

A surprising contrast to the medieval charm of Assisi, the Galleria d'Arte Contemporanea showcases modern interpretations of themes deeply rooted in the city's identity. I recall being captivated by an abstract installation representing St. Francis' connection to nature.

If you're into photography or sculptures, there are often seasonal exhibits by Italian and international artists. Spend at least an hour here to explore the blend of old and new, and consider ending your visit with a coffee at a nearby café—it's a wonderful way to reflect.

5. Museo della Porziuncola

- **Address:** Piazza Porziuncola, 1, 06081 Santa Maria degli Angeli, Assisi PG, Italy
- **Contact:** +39 075 805141
- **Website:** www.porziuncola.org
- **Opening Hours:** 9:00 AM
- **Closing Hours:** 7:00 PM
- **Admission Fee:** €8
- **Special Exhibits:** Artifacts and relics from the Basilica of Santa Maria degli Angeli
- **Directions:** A short drive from Assisi's city center, located in Santa Maria degli Angeli.

The Museo della Porziuncola was a spiritual highlight for me. Situated near the Basilica of Santa Maria degli Angeli, this museum houses relics, manuscripts, and stunning artworks tied to St. Francis and the Franciscan order. The Porziuncola itself—a tiny chapel—is a masterpiece of devotion and humility.

The museum also offers a small but poignant exhibit about the life of St. Francis. Give yourself at least 2 hours here, as there's a lot to take in. Don't miss the serene gardens outside—they're perfect for quiet contemplation.

6. Museo Diocesano e Cripta di San Rufino

- **Address:** Piazza San Rufino, 3, 06081 Assisi PG, Italy
- **Contact:** +39 075 812712
- **Website:** www.diocesiassisi.it
- **Opening Hours:** 10:00 AM
- **Closing Hours:** 6:00 PM
- **Admission Fee:** €7
- **Special Exhibits:** Archaeological finds and religious art
- **Directions:** Located near the Cathedral of San Rufino, just off Via San Rufino.

The Diocesan Museum and Crypt of San Rufino is another hidden gem. I was struck by the mosaics and intricate stone carvings in the crypt. The museum above houses religious artifacts and artwork from various periods, including some stunning 12th-century pieces.

Plan for about 1.5 hours here, especially if you enjoy archaeological sites. It's a bit off the beaten path, which means fewer crowds and a more intimate experience.

7. Museo del Tesoro della Basilica di San Francesco

- **Address:** Piazza San Francesco, 2, 06081 Assisi PG, Italy
- **Contact:** +39 075 819001
- **Website:** www.sanfrancescoassisi.org
- **Opening Hours:** 9:00 AM
- **Closing Hours:** 5:00 PM

- **Admission Fee:** €10 (includes the Basilica tour)
- **Special Exhibits:** Rare manuscripts and sacred treasures
- **Directions:** Inside the Basilica of San Francesco complex.

I saved the best for last. The Museo del Tesoro is a treasure trove—literally. It holds manuscripts, reliquaries, and sacred objects that highlight the Basilica's historical importance. One of the most impressive items was an illuminated manuscript dating back to the 13th century.

Take at least 2-3 hours to explore the museum and Basilica. Don't rush—this is a place where every corner holds something remarkable. And trust me, catching the golden hour light outside the Basilica is an experience in itself.

8. Museo Civico (Civic Museum)

- **Address:** Via Portica, 2, 06081 Assisi PG, Italy
- **Contact:** +39 075 813091
- **Website:** www.museocivicoassisi.it
- **Opening Hours:** 9:30 AM
- **Closing Hours:** 5:30 PM
- **Admission Fee:** €4
- **Special Exhibits:** Roman and medieval artifacts
- **Directions:** Located near Piazza del Comune, a short walk from the Roman Temple of Minerva.

The Museo Civico is tucked away but worth every step. I stumbled upon it while exploring the streets near Piazza del Comune. Inside, I found an eclectic collection of Roman and medieval artifacts, including pottery, tools, and jewelry. One of the highlights for me was the restored Roman frescoes—they're breathtakingly vivid.

This museum is compact but packed with history. Plan for an hour, and be sure to chat with the staff—they're happy to share interesting anecdotes about the exhibits.

9. Museo della Scuola

- **Address:** Via San Rufino, 15, 06081 Assisi PG, Italy
- **Contact:** +39 075 813012
- **Website:** www.museodellascuolaassisi.it
- **Opening Hours:** 10:00 AM
- **Closing Hours:** 6:00 PM
- **Admission Fee:** €5
- **Special Exhibits:** Vintage school artifacts and teaching materials
- **Directions:** A short walk from the Cathedral of San Rufino, along Via San Rufino.

The Museo della Scuola is one of Assisi's most charming finds. It's a nostalgic tribute to early 20th-century education, with vintage desks, textbooks, and even uniforms on display. Visiting felt like stepping into a classroom from a century ago, complete with wooden benches and chalkboards.

If you have children or a soft spot for history, this museum offers a delightful experience. Spend about an hour here to enjoy the quirky exhibits and relive a piece of the past.

10. Museo Missionario Indios Frati Cappuccini (Capuchin Missionary Museum)

- **Address:** Via Santuario delle Carceri, 18, 06081 Assisi PG, Italy

- **Contact:** +39 075 802076
- **Website:** www.missionarymuseumassisi.it
- **Opening Hours:** 10:00 AM
- **Closing Hours:** 6:00 PM
- **Admission Fee:** Free (donations welcome)
- **Special Exhibits:** Artifacts and stories from Capuchin missions worldwide
- **Directions:** Located on the road to Eremo delle Carceri, about a 15-minute drive from the town center.

This museum took me by surprise with its unique collection. It showcases artifacts from Capuchin missionary expeditions to South America and Africa, including indigenous tools, clothing, and artwork. What struck me most was the personal stories of the missionaries, detailed through letters and photographs.

It's a small museum, but you can spend an hour or more exploring. It's also a great stop on your way to Eremo delle Carceri, offering a different perspective on Assisi's global connections.

11. Casa di Properzio

- **Address:** Via del Torrione, 06081 Assisi PG, Italy
- **Contact:** +39 075 812862
- **Opening Hours:** 10:00 AM
- **Closing Hours:** 4:00 PM
- **Admission Fee:** €3
- **Special Exhibits:** Roman mosaics and ancient architecture
- **Directions:** Near Porta Perlici, on the northern side of the city.

The Casa di Properzio is an archaeological site often overlooked by visitors. It's a Roman-era domus with stunning mosaic floors and remnants of ancient architecture. I remember standing in awe of the intricate geometric patterns on the mosaics—they felt almost modern despite being centuries old.

This museum doesn't take long to visit (30-45 minutes), but it's a hidden gem for anyone fascinated by Roman history. Be sure to bring a camera—the mosaics are incredibly photogenic.

12. Museo del Vino (Wine Museum)

- **Address:** Via San Benedetto, 12, 06081 Assisi PG, Italy
- **Contact:** +39 075 8043770
- **Website:** www.museodelvinoassisi.it
- **Opening Hours:** 11:00 AM
- **Closing Hours:** 7:00 PM
- **Admission Fee:** €10 (includes wine tasting)
- **Special Exhibits:** History of winemaking in Umbria
- **Directions:** About 2 kilometers outside the city center, near several local vineyards.

As a wine enthusiast, this museum was a dream come true. It offers a fascinating look at the history and techniques of winemaking in the Umbria region. From ancient amphorae to modern equipment, it's a celebration of Assisi's deep connection to viticulture.

The best part? A complimentary wine tasting session at the end of your visit. I spent about 1.5 hours here, savoring both the exhibits and the wines. It's a must-visit for anyone who enjoys wine or wants to learn more about Assisi's agricultural heritage.

13. Museo del Tesoro di Santa Chiara (Treasure Museum of Santa Chiara)

- **Address:** Piazza Santa Chiara, 06081 Assisi PG, Italy
- **Contact:** +39 075 812282
- **Website:** www.santachiaraassisi.it
- **Opening Hours:** 9:00 AM
- **Closing Hours:** 5:00 PM
- **Admission Fee:** €6
- **Special Exhibits:** Relics and artifacts related to St. Clare
- **Directions:** Inside the Basilica of Santa Chiara, accessible from the main square.

This small museum within the Basilica of Santa Chiara is deeply spiritual. It houses relics of St. Clare and artifacts that provide insight into her life and the founding of the Poor Clares.

During my visit, I was especially drawn to her simple, handwoven garments—a humbling reminder of her commitment to humility. Plan for 30-45 minutes here, and make sure to spend some time in the basilica itself; its pink-and-white façade is one of Assisi's most iconic sights.

14. Museo delle Arti e Mestieri (Museum of Arts and Crafts)

- **Address:** Via San Paolo, 6, 06081 Assisi PG, Italy
- **Contact:** +39 075 812456
- **Opening Hours:** 9:30 AM
- **Closing Hours:** 5:30 PM
- **Admission Fee:** €5
- **Special Exhibits:** Traditional tools and crafts of Umbria
- **Directions:** Near the lower end of Via San Paolo, close to the Church of San Paolo.

For anyone curious about the everyday lives of Assisi's residents in centuries past, this museum is a gem. It features tools, textiles, and ceramics used by local artisans. I loved seeing the weaving looms and pottery wheels—they made me appreciate the craftsmanship behind the souvenirs sold in the city today.

Plan to spend about an hour here, especially if you enjoy hands-on learning. Some exhibits even allow visitors to try simple weaving techniques!

Off-the-Beaten-Path Attractions in Assisi

Assisi is renowned for its spiritual and historical richness, anchored by the Basilica of Saint Francis. Yet, for those willing to stray from the well-worn tourist paths, this enchanting Umbrian town has countless hidden gems waiting to be discovered. These lesser-known treasures reveal a deeper, more personal side of Assisi—a place where the spirit of the past thrives quietly, away from the crowds. Let me take you through a journey of these off-the-beaten-path attractions, drawing from personal experiences that made each visit unforgettable.

Hermitage of the Carceri

- **Location:** Via Eremo delle Carceri, 06081 Assisi PG, Italy
- **Why Visit:** A profound sense of solitude and spirituality

Nestled in the lush forest of Mount Subasio, the Hermitage of the Carceri is a sanctuary that feels worlds away from the bustling streets of Assisi. I remember my first visit vividly—walking through the cool, shaded paths, I felt a sense of tranquility that's hard to describe. This hermitage was a retreat for Saint Francis and his followers, offering a glimpse into the ascetic life they embraced. As you explore the caves and chapels, the silence envelops you, broken only by birdsong—a poignant reminder of Francis' bond with nature.

San Damiano

- **Location:** Via San Damiano, 85, 06081 Assisi PG, Italy
- **Why Visit:** The cradle of the Franciscan movement

San Damiano is not just a site; it's a story etched in stone. This is where Saint Francis received his divine calling to "repair my church," inspiring him to begin his mission. When I first entered the humble chapel, I was struck by the simplicity and warmth of the place. It doesn't overwhelm like grand cathedrals; instead, it whispers stories of faith and humility. The cloistered gardens here were a favorite spot of Saint Clare and her sisters—a peaceful escape to reflect and soak in the beauty of creation.

Ponte dei Galli

- **Location:** Via Ponte dei Galli, 06081 Assisi PG, Italy
- **Why Visit:** A medieval bridge and a scenic retreat

Ponte dei Galli, a charming medieval bridge just outside the town, offers an unexpected slice of serenity. This is where I stumbled upon Assisi's countryside charm—an easy walk but far from any crowds. With the backdrop of Mount Subasio and fields that seem to stretch endlessly, the bridge provides a perfect spot for reflection or a quiet picnic. It felt like stepping into a postcard, with its unspoiled beauty and the soothing sound of water flowing beneath.

Temple of Minerva's Crypt

- **Location:** Piazza del Comune, 06081 Assisi PG, Italy
- **Why Visit:** Layers of ancient Roman history

You've likely walked past the Temple of Minerva in Assisi's central square, but have you ventured beneath it? I nearly missed this one myself until a local shopkeeper tipped me off. Descending into the crypt, you're transported back to Roman times. The remnants of pagan worship blend seamlessly with early Christian influences, creating a space that feels almost suspended in time. It's humbling to stand in a place that has witnessed millennia of change, yet still holds onto its essence.

Santa Maria delle Rose

- **Location:** Via Santa Maria delle Rose, 10, 06081 Assisi PG, Italy
- **Why Visit:** A hidden art haven in a forgotten church

Walking through the narrow lanes of Assisi, I stumbled upon the unassuming Santa Maria delle Rose. Inside, an unexpected world of contemporary art and spiritual installations unfolds. The church itself, no longer used for worship, has been transformed into an art space that bridges the ancient and modern. One installation, a cascade of rose petals, was so mesmerizing that I sat there for ages, soaking in the ambiance. This is not your typical Assisi experience, but that's exactly why it's special.

Basilica of Santa Maria degli Angeli (Porziuncola)

- **Location:** Piazza Porziuncola, 1, 06081 Assisi PG, Italy

- **Why Visit:** A spiritual epicenter often overlooked

While technically not in the heart of Assisi, the Basilica of Santa Maria degli Angeli is an essential detour. Inside this grand basilica lies the tiny chapel of Porziuncola, where Saint Francis founded the Franciscan Order. The contrast between the ornate basilica and the simple chapel is striking, and I found myself drawn to the latter. The atmosphere here is charged with history and devotion, a place where you can almost feel the weight of the Franciscan legacy.

Bosco di San Francesco

- **Location:** Via Ponte dei Galli, 06081 Assisi PG, Italy
- **Why Visit:** A natural escape infused with Franciscan philosophy

The Bosco di San Francesco, a nature reserve managed by FAI (Fondo Ambiente Italiano), is more than a forest—it's a journey through Franciscan values. I followed the winding trails down into the valley, passing through olive groves, meadows, and ancient ruins. At the end of the path, the Land Art installation by Michelangelo Pistoletto, "The Third Paradise," was a delightful surprise. Walking this trail felt like stepping into Saint Francis' worldview—one of harmony with nature and simplicity.

Assisi Underground

- **Location:** Various sites beneath Assisi's historic center
- **Why Visit:** Explore the city's ancient Roman roots

Assisi Underground offers a chance to peel back the layers of history. Beneath the medieval streets, you'll find remnants of Roman houses, roads, and even an amphitheater. Guided tours take you through these subterranean treasures, and I found it fascinating to see how seamlessly the past and present coexist. It's a reminder of Assisi's long-standing importance and resilience through the ages.

Monte Subasio Trails

- **Location:** Accessible from various trailheads around Assisi
- **Why Visit:** Breathtaking views and natural serenity

Monte Subasio, the mountain that cradles Assisi, offers hiking trails that reveal a different side of the town. I took an early morning trek here and was rewarded with sweeping views of the Umbrian valley, bathed in golden light. The trails are well-marked and range from easy walks to more challenging hikes. Along the way, you'll encounter wildflowers, ancient trees, and the occasional glimpse of wildlife. It's an ideal way to connect with the natural beauty that Saint Francis cherished.

Rivotorto Sanctuary

- **Location:** Rivotorto, 06081 Assisi PG, Italy
- **Why Visit:** A humble shrine to Franciscan beginnings

Just a short drive from Assisi, the Rivotorto Sanctuary is often overlooked in favor of its more famous counterparts. Yet, this small shrine holds immense historical significance—it was here that Saint Francis and his companions lived in poverty before receiving Porziuncola. The simple structure reflects their humble beginnings, and visiting felt like stepping into the roots of the Franciscan story. I sat on one of the benches, imagining the camaraderie and determination of those early days.

The Rocca Minore

- **Location:** Via della Rocca, 06081 Assisi PG, Italy
- **Why Visit:** Stunning views and a touch of medieval adventure

While most visitors climb up to the Rocca Maggiore, fewer make the effort to explore the smaller Rocca Minore. Perched on a nearby hill, this fortress offers equally breathtaking views of Assisi and the surrounding landscape, without the crowds. The climb can be steep, but the solitude and sweeping panoramas make it worth every step. I spent a peaceful afternoon here, enjoying the sense of being removed from the hustle below.

Abbazia di San Benedetto al Subasio

- **Location:** Strada Comunale di San Benedetto, 06081 Assisi PG, Italy
- **Why Visit:** Ancient ruins with a serene mountain backdrop

This hidden abbey, perched on the slopes of Mount Subasio, is a treasure for history buffs and nature lovers alike. I stumbled upon it during a leisurely walk, and the atmosphere was captivating. The ruins of this 10th-century Benedictine monastery whisper tales of monastic life, blending seamlessly with the surrounding natural beauty. The quiet here is profound, and the abbey feels almost forgotten—a perfect spot for meditation or simply soaking in the peaceful surroundings.

Oratorio dei Pellegrini

- **Location:** Via San Francesco, 13, 06081 Assisi PG, Italy
- **Why Visit:** A small chapel with stunning frescoes

While wandering Assisi's cobblestone streets, I nearly passed by this unassuming oratory. Its plain exterior belies the artistic treasures within—vivid frescoes that recount the lives of Saint James and Saint Anthony. The artwork is intimate and detailed, offering a glimpse into the devotional practices of pilgrims who visited Assisi centuries ago. This tiny chapel feels like a step back in time, and the quietude inside makes it all the more special.

Fonte Oliviera

- **Location:** Viale Giovanna di Savoia, 06081 Assisi PG, Italy
- **Why Visit:** A historic fountain tucked away from tourist trails

This little-known fountain, hidden along a quiet road, is a slice of Assisi's medieval past. I stumbled upon it while exploring the outskirts of the city. The fountain, shaded by olive trees, is a remnant of a bygone era when it served as a watering spot for pilgrims and locals. Its cool, refreshing waters are still a welcome respite, and the surrounding serenity makes it a perfect place for a reflective pause.

Castelnuovo di Assisi

- **Location:** Castelnuovo, 06081 Assisi PG, Italy

- **Why Visit:** A charming medieval village just minutes from Assisi

A short drive from Assisi's center brought me to Castelnuovo, a quaint village that seems frozen in time. Its narrow streets, ancient walls, and friendly locals immediately charmed me. Unlike the bustling center of Assisi, Castelnuovo feels untouched by tourism. I spent a delightful afternoon wandering its quiet lanes, stopping at a small café for a cappuccino, and chatting with residents who shared stories of their beloved home.

Santuario Madonna dei Tre Fossi

- **Location:** Via del Caminaccio, 06081 Assisi PG, Italy
- **Why Visit:** A serene sanctuary with stunning countryside views

This tiny sanctuary, nestled among rolling hills, is a peaceful retreat. I visited on a recommendation from a local and was amazed by its simplicity and beauty. The church is small but beautifully adorned, and the surrounding landscape offers panoramic views of the Umbrian valley. It's a place where you can sit on a stone bench, listen to the rustle of olive trees, and let the beauty of Assisi's countryside wash over you.

Parco della Mola di Campello

- **Location:** Campello sul Clitunno, 06042 Perugia PG, Italy
- **Why Visit:** A tranquil park with natural springs and medieval ruins

Though slightly outside Assisi, this park is worth the short trip. The Mola di Campello is a hidden oasis, where crystal-clear springs bubble up from the earth. Walking through the park, I came across medieval mills and ancient ruins, each telling stories of a time when the area bustled with activity. I loved the feeling of walking through a place that blends natural beauty with historical significance.

Convento di San Giovanni Battista

- **Location:** Località Costa di Trex, 06081 Assisi PG, Italy
- **Why Visit:** A remote convent with stunning views and historical charm

This convent, perched high in the hills near Assisi, is a true hidden gem. I found it during a hiking excursion, and it felt like discovering a secret treasure. The convent is a testament to the simple life of its former residents, and its location offers breathtaking views of the valley below. Though it's a bit of a climb to reach, the serenity and panoramic vistas make it well worth the effort.

Chiesa di Santa Croce

- **Location:** Via Santa Croce, 06081 Assisi PG, Italy
- **Why Visit:** A quiet, unassuming church with deep spiritual roots

Tucked away in a quiet corner of Assisi, the Chiesa di Santa Croce is a modest church with a rich history. It's said to have been built on the site of an earlier Christian settlement. I was struck by the peaceful ambiance here—it feels far removed from the grandeur of

Assisi's more famous churches, but its simplicity and authenticity give it a unique charm. Inside, you'll find a few beautiful frescoes that echo the town's spiritual essence.

Via degli Archi

- **Location:** Connecting various parts of Assisi's old town
- **Why Visit:** A picturesque medieval street with hidden courtyards

This narrow street winds its way through Assisi's medieval heart, offering delightful surprises at every turn. I loved wandering along Via degli Archi and stumbling upon hidden courtyards, small artisan shops, and quiet corners where time seemed to stand still. The arches that line the street are a photographer's dream, framing Assisi's rustic beauty in unexpected ways. It's the kind of place you'd only find by getting lost—and that's the best way to explore Assisi.

Pieve di Santa Maria di Lignano

- **Location:** Località Lignano, 06081 Assisi PG, Italy
- **Why Visit:** A beautifully preserved rural church in the Umbrian countryside

This small rural church is tucked away in the hills outside Assisi, surrounded by lush greenery. Visiting felt like stepping back in time—its Romanesque architecture and tranquil setting exude an old-world charm. The journey here, through winding country roads, is as enchanting as the destination itself. I attended a small, local event here once, and the sense of community was heartwarming.

Torre del Popolo

- **Location:** Piazza del Comune, 06081 Assisi PG, Italy
- **Why Visit:** A climb with rewarding panoramic views

Many people overlook the Torre del Popolo, focusing instead on the nearby Temple of Minerva. But this medieval tower offers one of the best views of Assisi and the surrounding countryside. The climb is steep, but the vista from the top is unforgettable. Standing there, with the town's rooftops sprawling below and the green valleys stretching to the horizon, I felt an incredible connection to the history and beauty of Assisi.

CHAPTER 6: PRACTICAL INFORMATION

Safety and Security Considerations

Safety and security are vital aspects to consider when exploring a destination like Assisi, a place renowned for its spiritual essence, historical significance, and serene beauty. Walking through its cobblestone streets, you can't help but feel an overwhelming sense of calm, almost as if the city itself is watching over you. But like any other destination, being mindful of your surroundings and taking a few precautions ensures that your trip remains as peaceful as the town itself.

When I first arrived in Assisi, I was struck by how safe it felt. The town has a unique atmosphere—partly because it attracts pilgrims and travelers who are often more respectful and conscientious. The locals are warm and welcoming, and there's a real sense of community. That said, I quickly realized that feeling safe shouldn't lead to complacency, especially when you're traveling. Even in a place as tranquil as Assisi, it's always wise to stay aware.

One thing I noticed right away is that Assisi is a walking town. Its steep hills and narrow streets aren't made for rushing. I remember wandering up towards the Basilica of St. Francis and feeling a bit winded but so immersed in the experience. While the streets are generally safe, they can be quite slippery when it rains. A local shopkeeper warned me to watch my step on the polished cobblestones—advice I was grateful for when I nearly slipped during a sudden downpour. Comfortable, sturdy shoes are a must here, and paying attention to where you're stepping is as much about safety as it is about soaking in the beauty of your surroundings.

During my stay, I found that Assisi has a low crime rate, but like any tourist spot, it's not entirely free of petty theft. Crowds gather around popular landmarks like the Basilica of St. Francis, especially during religious festivals or peak tourist seasons. It's in these bustling moments that you should keep a close eye on your belongings. I always kept my bag zipped and held close to my body, particularly in areas where I found myself absorbed in the awe-inspiring architecture and art. It's easy to get distracted here—the frescoes alone are enough to transport you to another world.

Nighttime in Assisi is magical, with the streets illuminated by soft, golden lights. There's a different kind of tranquility in the air after the day's crowds have dispersed. I felt entirely comfortable walking around after dark, but it's always a good idea to stick to well-lit areas and avoid wandering into unfamiliar or deserted parts of town. Not that there are many dark alleys in Assisi—most paths eventually lead to a piazza or a landmark—but being cautious is never a bad idea.

Public transportation in and around Assisi is reliable, but taxis are a bit of a luxury here. If you're traveling alone and returning late from a nearby town, I'd recommend booking your transport in advance. I remember coming back from a day trip to Perugia and realizing too late that the buses weren't as frequent in the evening. Thankfully, a friendly local pointed me toward a reliable taxi service, but the whole experience reminded me to plan ahead. It's these small things—checking schedules, knowing your options—that make travel in Assisi feel smoother and safer.

I also learned to be cautious with my phone and wallet when stopping for a coffee or gelato. The cafes and trattorias near Piazza del Comune are so charming that you might forget the basics of keeping your valuables secure. I once left my phone on a table outside a café while paying inside, and though nothing happened, it was a reminder to always be mindful. The locals are kind and honest, but you can't always account for everyone in a tourist-heavy area.

Another aspect of safety in Assisi is health-related. The town is perched on a hill, and getting from one place to another often involves a fair bit of walking uphill or climbing stairs. While it's fantastic exercise and part of the charm, it can be tiring, especially on hot summer days. I remember feeling completely drained one afternoon and realized I hadn't been drinking enough water. There are fountains scattered around the town where you can refill your bottle, but staying hydrated is crucial. If you're visiting during summer, sunscreen and a hat are lifesavers. The sun can be surprisingly strong even in the shaded streets.

Speaking of health, it's comforting to know that Assisi has good medical facilities for a small town. While I didn't need to visit a doctor, I always make it a point to research the nearest clinics and pharmacies when I travel. Pharmacies in Italy are easy to recognize—they have a green cross sign—and the pharmacists are knowledgeable and helpful. It's a small step, but knowing where to go in case of an emergency added an extra layer of peace of mind during my trip.

When it comes to food and drink safety, Assisi didn't give me much to worry about. The local cuisine is fresh, flavorful, and prepared with care. I enjoyed hearty plates of pasta and local wines without any concern. That said, it's always a good idea to stick to bottled water if you're unsure about the tap water in a foreign country. In Assisi, the water was perfectly fine, but I opted for bottled just to be cautious.

One of the most reassuring aspects of my visit was the presence of police and local authorities. You'll often see them around the main squares and landmarks, offering assistance and maintaining a visible presence. It's not intrusive at all, but rather a reminder that safety is taken seriously here. I had a brief chat with one officer near the Basilica, who was happy to give directions and even recommend a quieter spot to enjoy the sunset. Their approachability added to the overall sense of security.

Traveling solo in Assisi, I found it helpful to let someone know my plans for the day, especially when I ventured into the countryside or took less-traveled paths. Mobile reception in and around Assisi is generally good, but there are a few spots where it might drop, especially in more rural areas. Having an offline map downloaded on my phone was a lifesaver when I decided to explore the hiking trails around Mount Subasio. It's a breathtaking area, but the trails can be confusing if you're not paying attention.

I also made a habit of carrying a small daypack with essentials like a power bank, snacks, and a lightweight scarf for sudden temperature changes. Assisi's weather can be unpredictable, with mornings feeling crisp and afternoons turning warm, so dressing in layers was another tip I picked up quickly.

One final piece of advice that stuck with me is to respect the local customs and traditions. Assisi is a deeply spiritual town, and its residents take their faith and heritage seriously. I noticed this especially in places like the Basilica of St. Francis and Santa Maria degli Angeli. Dressing modestly when entering religious sites and maintaining a respectful demeanor isn't just courteous—it's a way of blending in and showing appreciation for the culture.

In the end, my time in Assisi felt like an effortless blend of safety and serenity. The town invites you to slow down, to reflect, and to immerse yourself in its timeless beauty. With just a little mindfulness and preparation, you can let go of any worries and simply enjoy everything Assisi has to offer. Walking through its streets, watching the sunset from Rocca Maggiore, or simply savoring a quiet moment in one of its piazzas—you'll find that safety here is almost a natural state of being. It's a place that holds you gently, encouraging you to explore with both curiosity and care.

Money Matters and Currency Exchange

Assisi, a gem tucked away in the heart of Italy, invites visitors with its charming streets, ancient architecture, and a spiritual aura that resonates throughout the town. Walking through its cobbled alleys, one feels a profound connection to its rich history, but alongside the charm of discovery comes the practical side of travel—understanding the nuances of money matters and currency exchange in a foreign land. Let me share with you some insights based on my experience, which might make your visit smoother and more enjoyable.

As you prepare for your trip to Assisi, one of the first things to consider is how you will manage your money. Italy uses the euro, and it's essential to arrive with at least a small amount of cash in euros. When I first planned my trip, I underestimated how useful cash would be in a small town like Assisi. Although cards are widely accepted in larger cities, Assisi's quaint shops, local eateries, and markets often prefer cash. I vividly remember entering a charming little shop filled with artisanal olive oils and handmade pottery. The elderly shopkeeper had a cash-only policy, which caught me off guard. Thankfully, there was an ATM nearby, and I quickly resolved the issue, but it taught me the value of always having some euros on hand.

Speaking of ATMs, they are conveniently scattered throughout Assisi, especially near the main tourist spots. I found one right next to the Basilica of St. Francis, which was a lifesaver after indulging in a spontaneous shopping spree for rosaries and local wine. However, a word of caution—be mindful of fees. Depending on your bank, you might face foreign transaction charges and withdrawal fees. Before my trip, I made sure to check with my bank about international ATM partnerships to minimize extra costs. Some banks even refund ATM fees, which can add up if you're withdrawing money frequently.

Currency exchange is another aspect to consider. While it's possible to exchange money at airports or in major cities before heading to Assisi, the rates aren't always favorable. I learned this the hard way at Fiumicino Airport in Rome, where the exchange rate left much to be desired. Once in Assisi, I found that local banks and exchange offices offered slightly better rates, but they often had limited hours of operation. This is something to keep in mind if you're arriving late in the evening or during a holiday. Planning ahead can save you both time and money.

If you're thinking about using credit or debit cards, rest assured that most mid-to-high-end restaurants and accommodations in Assisi accept them. However, I noticed that smaller trattorias and family-run establishments often preferred cash. During one particularly memorable meal at a cozy trattoria overlooking the Umbrian hills, I realized they didn't take cards just as the bill arrived. It wasn't a problem since I had euros with me, but it was a gentle reminder to always double-check payment options before sitting down.

One aspect I appreciated about Assisi was how locals approach transactions with warmth and patience. Even during a bustling afternoon at the Piazza del Comune, the vendors were kind enough to wait while I sorted out my payment, and one even gave me a quick lesson in counting euro coins. Moments like these not only eased the stress of dealing with a foreign currency but also added a touch of humanity to the experience.

For those who prefer contactless payments, I found that it's a growing trend in Italy, but it's not as prevalent in smaller towns like Assisi compared to big cities like Rome or Milan. My card worked flawlessly in most of the souvenir shops and at the entrance to the basilicas. Yet, there were instances, such as at a countryside vineyard tour, where cash was king. It's a good idea to carry a mix of payment options to cover all bases.

Budgeting for Assisi is another aspect where I learned a few tricks. Despite being a popular tourist destination, Assisi offers plenty of affordable options. A simple yet delicious meal of pasta and a glass of wine at a local trattoria cost me much less than I anticipated. However, I did splurge on guided tours and entrance fees to some of the basilicas, which were worth every penny. If you're visiting during one of the town's famous religious festivals, keep in mind that prices for accommodation and services might spike due to increased demand. Booking in advance and setting aside a little extra cash for such occasions can make a big difference.

One delightful discovery I made was how far a little money could go in Assisi when it came to local goods. From fragrant lavender sachets to intricately crafted ceramics, the town is a treasure trove for unique souvenirs. However, bargaining isn't a common practice here, unlike in some other parts of the world. Prices are generally fair, and the artisans take great pride in their work. That said, I found that paying in cash sometimes earned me a small discount or a friendly smile of appreciation from the vendor.

Tipping in Assisi is another area where I had some questions initially. While tipping isn't as customary in Italy as it is in countries like the United States, it's always appreciated. In restaurants, rounding up the bill or leaving a few euros for excellent service is a thoughtful gesture. When I left a small tip after a particularly memorable meal, the owner came over to personally thank me, which made the experience even more special.

For those planning a longer stay or frequent travels to Europe, it might be worth considering a multi-currency travel card. I used one during my trip, and it was incredibly convenient. It allowed me to lock in exchange rates before traveling, which gave me peace of mind knowing I wouldn't be affected by sudden currency fluctuations. Reloading the card was straightforward, and it worked seamlessly across ATMs and card terminals in Assisi.

One final piece of advice I'd offer is to always carry a mix of small and large denominations. I learned this lesson during a visit to a local bakery, where the shopkeeper didn't have enough change for a €50 note. Since then, I made it a point to keep smaller bills and coins for such occasions. It's a small habit, but it made day-to-day transactions much smoother.

Looking back, managing money in Assisi was less about strict planning and more about being adaptable. The town's laid-back vibe and the kindness of its people made even the occasional hiccup a minor inconvenience. Whether it was enjoying a cappuccino at a sunlit café or purchasing a handmade memento, every transaction felt like a part of the larger story of my journey.

As you prepare for your own adventure in Assisi, my biggest takeaway is this: embrace the simplicity and charm of the town, and let that guide your approach to money matters. With a little preparation and an open mind, you'll find that navigating currency and finances becomes just another delightful part of the experience. And who knows? You might even come away with your own stories to share about those unforgettable moments when euros changed hands under the timeless Umbrian sky.

Transportation & Getting Around in Assisi

Getting around Assisi, a charming town in Italy's Umbria region, is both a delightful and practical experience. With its medieval streets, picturesque landscapes, and historic landmarks, transportation here isn't just a means to an end; it's part of the journey. Let me guide you through the options you'll have when visiting this quaint yet well-connected town. I'll share the details in a way that feels like we're sitting together over coffee, talking about your upcoming trip.

Public Bus

The public bus network in Assisi is surprisingly efficient, given its small-town vibe. Most of the buses are run by Umbria Mobilità, which connects key areas within Assisi and surrounding towns like Santa Maria degli Angeli and Perugia.

- **Routes**: The main route you'll likely use is the one that connects the train station at Santa Maria degli Angeli to the upper town, where most of Assisi's iconic sites, such as the Basilica of St. Francis, are located. It's a steep climb up to the old town, so this bus is a godsend if you're not in the mood to trek uphill. Other routes serve nearby towns and rural areas, which are perfect if you want to explore beyond Assisi's main attractions.
- **Fare**: A single bus ticket costs around €1.50 if you buy it in advance at a tabaccheria (tobacco shop) or kiosk, or €2 if purchased directly on the bus. It's worth getting your tickets beforehand to save a bit of money and avoid fumbling for change on the bus.
- **Operating Hours**: Most buses start running around 6:30 AM and operate until about 10 PM, though service is less frequent in the evenings. It's always a good idea to check the schedule posted at bus stops to avoid long waits.
- **Card/Token System**: If you're staying for a few days and plan to use public transport often, consider getting a multi-ride card. It's easy to load and saves you from buying individual tickets each time.

From personal experience, I found the buses reliable and clean, but they can get crowded during peak tourist season. Pro tip: Try to grab a window seat if you can. The views of Assisi's surrounding hills and olive groves as you ascend into the old town are breathtaking.

Walking

Honestly, my favorite way to get around Assisi is on foot. The old town is compact, and the narrow cobblestone streets invite you to slow down and soak in the medieval atmosphere. You'll pass charming shops, quiet courtyards, and little cafes where you can grab a cappuccino or gelato.

- **Routes**: If you're fit enough to handle some inclines, you can walk almost everywhere within the old town. The Basilica of St. Francis, Piazza del Comune, and the Rocca Maggiore fortress are all easily accessible on foot. I also recommend wandering without a strict itinerary; you never know what hidden gem you might stumble upon.
- **Fare**: Free! Unless you count the calories burned and the gelato you'll reward yourself with afterward.
- **Operating Hours**: Anytime your legs are up for it. However, be cautious at night as some areas can be dimly lit, though Assisi is generally very safe.

One thing I'll say: Wear comfortable shoes. Cobblestones are not your friend if you're in flip-flops or heels. Trust me on this—I learned the hard way after an ambitious day of sightseeing.

Taxis

Taxis in Assisi are a good option if you're traveling with luggage or need to get somewhere in a hurry, but they're not the most economical choice for daily transportation.

- **Routes**: You can hail a taxi at the train station, Piazza del Comune, or near major attractions. If you're staying at a hotel, the front desk can also call one for you.

- **Fare**: A short ride within town will cost around €10–€15, while longer trips to nearby villages or back to the train station might run €20–€30. Fares can add up, so taxis are best reserved for specific needs.
- **Operating Hours**: Taxis operate 24/7, but availability can be hit-or-miss late at night or in the early morning. Always book in advance if you have an early train or flight to catch.

While I didn't use taxis often during my visit, they were a lifesaver when I arrived with heavy luggage and just wanted to get to my accommodation without fuss. Be aware that tipping isn't obligatory in Italy, but rounding up to the nearest euro is appreciated.

Private Car or Car Rentals

If you're planning to explore the Umbrian countryside or nearby towns like Spello, Perugia, or Montefalco, renting a car can be a game-changer.

- **Routes**: Driving in Assisi itself can be tricky due to limited traffic zones (ZTL) in the historic center. Only residents and authorized vehicles are allowed to drive through these areas, so you'll need to park outside the town walls. The parking lots at Mojano, Giovanni Paolo II, and Matteotti are convenient and have shuttle services that take you into the old town.
- **Fare**: Car rentals typically cost €40–€60 per day for a small car, plus the cost of fuel, which is about €1.85 per liter. Parking fees range from €1–€2 per hour, depending on the lot.
- **Operating Hours**: Rental agencies usually operate from 8:30 AM to 6 PM, but some offer 24/7 drop-off options.

Driving through the rolling hills of Umbria was one of my favorite experiences. The roads are well-maintained, and the views of vineyards, sunflower fields, and ancient stone villages are postcard-perfect. Just make sure you have a good GPS or download offline maps because rural areas can have spotty service.

Bicycles and E-Bikes

For those who enjoy a more active way to explore, bicycles and e-bikes are becoming increasingly popular in Assisi.

- **Routes**: You can ride through the lower parts of Assisi and into the countryside. The trail connecting Santa Maria degli Angeli to Spello is particularly scenic, with gentle slopes and stunning views.
- **Fare**: Regular bicycles can be rented for about €10–€15 per day, while e-bikes cost around €30–€40 per day. Some hotels also offer free or discounted rentals for guests.
- **Operating Hours**: Rentals are typically available from morning until early evening. Check with local shops for specific timings.

I tried an e-bike for the first time here, and it was a game-changer. The assist made climbing hills a breeze, and I still got to enjoy the open air and stunning scenery without breaking too much of a sweat. It's a fantastic way to venture further afield while staying eco-friendly.

Shuttles

Assisi offers convenient shuttle buses that connect key points like parking lots and major attractions.

- **Routes**: The most useful shuttle route is the one that connects the parking lots (e.g., Mojano, Giovanni Paolo II) to Piazza del Comune and other parts of the old town.
- **Fare**: Tickets cost around €1–€1.50 per ride or €3 for a daily pass, which allows unlimited rides.
- **Operating Hours**: Shuttles usually run from 7 AM to 10 PM but may have extended hours during festivals or peak tourist season.

These shuttles are incredibly handy, especially if you've parked outside the old town. I loved using them on hot afternoons when the uphill walk felt a bit too daunting.

Trains

While trains won't help you get around within Assisi, they're your best bet for arriving in town or exploring nearby destinations.

- **Routes**: The train station is located in Santa Maria degli Angeli, about 4 km (2.5 miles) from the old town. Frequent trains connect Assisi to Rome, Florence, Perugia, and other major cities.
- **Fare**: Tickets to Perugia cost around €3–€5, while a trip to Rome or Florence will set you back €15–€25, depending on the type of train.
- **Operating Hours**: Trains run from early morning until late evening, with some routes offering high-speed options for quicker travel.

I arrived in Assisi by train and found it incredibly convenient. From the station, you can catch a bus or taxi to reach the historic center.

Health Precautions

Assisi is a place that feels as though it belongs to another time—its cobbled streets, ancient architecture, and serene atmosphere make it a destination that soothes the soul. Yet, like with any journey, it's essential to be prepared and aware of the health precautions you should take when visiting this historic gem. Let me share my insights, not from a guidebook, but from the lens of someone who has wandered those picturesque streets and breathed in the crisp Umbrian air.

One of the first things I realized about Assisi was how much walking it involves. The town is built on a hill, and that means you'll be climbing inclines and navigating uneven pathways. While this adds to its charm, it's a workout—especially if you're not accustomed to it. Wearing comfortable footwear is more than just a suggestion here; it's a necessity. On my first visit, I naively wore sandals with little support, thinking they'd suit the warm weather. By the end of the day, my feet ached, and I found myself desperately hunting for a pharmacy to buy some gel inserts. Trust me, invest in sturdy, supportive shoes.

The weather in Assisi can be deceptively pleasant. In the summer, the sun can be intense, reflecting off the pale stone of the buildings. While it's tempting to linger outside soaking in the beauty, it's easy to underestimate how much time you've spent under the sun. I learned the hard way when I forgot to reapply sunscreen after a morning stroll. By mid-afternoon, I had a rosy reminder of my mistake. Always carry sunscreen with you and, if possible, wear a hat or use an umbrella for shade. Even in cooler months, the sun can catch you off guard, especially since the air often feels crisp and cool.

When it comes to hydration, it's another lesson I absorbed quite literally. Exploring Assisi means a lot of walking and climbing, and staying hydrated is key. The town has several fountains with drinkable water, and these were lifesavers for me. Carrying a reusable water bottle turned out to be one of the smartest things I did. The water in Assisi is fresh and safe to drink, and refilling at these fountains not only kept me hydrated but also added a sense of connection to the town's rhythm.

Food is one of Assisi's great joys, but like anywhere, it's worth being mindful of your choices. I remember my first meal there vividly—a plate of strangozzi pasta with truffles that was both simple and divine. However, I also recall being so tempted by street vendors selling all sorts of goodies that I probably pushed my limits. While most establishments and vendors in Assisi are clean and reputable, it's wise to stick to places that look busy and have good turnover. A little vigilance goes a long way in avoiding any unpleasant surprises.

One thing I hadn't considered until I visited Assisi was how much the change in diet could affect me. Italian food, though delicious, can be quite rich, especially if you're indulging in the local delicacies like porchetta or cured meats. My stomach, unaccustomed to so much olive oil and cured ingredients, protested after a couple of days. Packing a small supply of antacids or digestive aids is a good idea, just in case your system takes time to adjust.

Speaking of adjustments, I cannot stress enough how important it is to have a small first aid kit with you. On one of my hikes to the Eremo delle Carceri, a hermitage just outside the town, I slipped on a mossy rock. It wasn't a major fall, but I ended up with a scrape on my knee. Having antiseptic wipes and a few bandages in my bag saved me from what could have been an inconvenient detour back to town. Even if you're not planning on hiking, the cobbled streets and uneven terrain in Assisi mean accidents can happen.

One aspect of health precautions that often goes overlooked is staying aware of your surroundings. Assisi's streets can get quite crowded, especially around landmarks like the Basilica of St. Francis. While the hustle and bustle are part of the charm, they can also be disorienting, and it's easy to lose your footing or bump into someone. Take your time, and don't rush through the narrow alleys. I remember being caught in a particularly crowded spot near the Piazza del Comune, and the press of the crowd made me feel a little lightheaded. Stepping aside and finding a quiet corner helped me regain my balance and composure.

If you have any specific medical needs or conditions, planning ahead is crucial. Assisi has a few pharmacies, but they don't carry everything you might be used to at home. During my stay, I developed a mild cold and was surprised to find that over-the-counter medications differed significantly from what I was accustomed to. The pharmacist was kind and helpful, but explaining symptoms with a language barrier was a challenge. If you rely on specific medications, bring enough to last your trip, along with a note from your doctor explaining their purpose, just in case customs has questions.

As with any travel, it's wise to have a basic understanding of the healthcare system in case of emergencies. Assisi is a small town, but it's well-connected to larger medical facilities in nearby Perugia. While I didn't need to use them, knowing where the nearest hospital was gave me peace of mind. If you're traveling with children or elderly family members, it's especially important to know what resources are available and how to access them.

Insect bites weren't something I initially associated with Assisi, but on a warm spring evening, while enjoying the view from Rocca Maggiore, the mosquitoes reminded me of their presence. A good insect repellent is something I now never travel without. It's a small addition to your bag but can make a big difference, especially if you're out during dusk.

Lastly, one of the most important health precautions is listening to your body. Assisi has a way of enchanting you, making you want to explore every corner and linger in every piazza. But it's easy to overdo it, especially if you're jet-lagged or simply not used to the level of activity. On one of my days there, I pushed myself too hard, trying to see everything in one go. By the evening, I was exhausted and ended up missing a dinner reservation because all I wanted to do was rest. Pace yourself, and remember that part of the joy of Assisi is soaking in its tranquil ambiance.

Traveling to Assisi is a journey that nourishes the soul, but being mindful of these health precautions ensures that your experience is as smooth and enjoyable as possible. It's a town that invites you to slow down, breathe deeply, and take in its beauty, but it's also a place that rewards those who come prepared. Whether you're marveling at the frescoes of Giotto, wandering the olive groves, or sipping a cappuccino in a sunlit square, a little foresight goes a long way in making your time in Assisi unforgettable.

Emergency contact numbers

Visiting Assisi is like stepping into a living masterpiece. The charming cobblestone streets, the serene aura of the Basilica of St. Francis, and the rolling Umbrian hills all make it a haven for travelers. But like any trip, it's essential to be prepared for unexpected situations. Knowing the emergency contact numbers and services in Assisi can bring peace of mind and help you navigate any challenges. Having been there myself, I can vouch for how reassuring it feels to have these details handy. Let me share what I learned, not just as a traveler but as someone who believes in being prepared.

Emergency Services: The Basics

First off, Italy uses the **112** universal emergency number. It's like the 911 equivalent in the United States or 999 in the UK. This number connects you to all major emergency services, including the police, ambulance, and fire department. What's comforting is that the operators often speak multiple languages, including English. I remember testing this out (purely out of curiosity, I assure you!) and found the process smooth and efficient.

When in Assisi, it's good to remember that local services work in tandem with the national ones. While 112 is your first go-to, knowing specific numbers for hospitals, police stations, and pharmacies can save valuable time.

Medical Emergencies in Assisi

Assisi's tranquil setting might make you feel invincible, but accidents and illnesses can happen anywhere. I caught a mild case of traveler's stomach after indulging in too much truffle pasta (a delicacy I absolutely don't regret). Fortunately, I had the medical emergency number handy: **118**.

- **118**: This is Italy's dedicated number for medical emergencies. It connects you directly to an ambulance service.

I also discovered that Assisi has a well-equipped medical center:

- **Ospedale di Assisi (Hospital of Assisi)**
    - **Address**: Via Valentin Muller, 06081 Assisi PG, Italy
    - **Phone**: +39 075 81391

During my visit, a friend of mine needed assistance for a minor sprain from hiking up to Rocca Maggiore (totally worth the climb, by the way). The hospital staff were friendly, professional, and patient despite the language barrier. They even recommended nearby pharmacies for follow-up care.

Police Assistance

Assisi is incredibly safe, but if you ever feel the need for police assistance—whether for a lost passport, theft, or directions—you can contact the local authorities. The number for the police is **113**.

- **Carabinieri (Military Police)**
    - **Phone**: 112 (also doubles as a general emergency number)
- **Polizia Municipale (Local Police)**
    - **Address**: Piazza del Comune, 06081 Assisi PG, Italy
    - **Phone**: +39 075 8138671

The local police office in Piazza del Comune was a familiar sight as I wandered the square. I stopped by to ask about traffic rules (you'll want to clarify if you're driving in the ZTL, or limited traffic zones). They were courteous and even helped me practice a bit of my broken Italian.

Fire Emergencies

While Assisi isn't exactly prone to raging fires, you never know when you might need to report one. Italy's fire brigade can be reached by dialing **115**.

- **Vigili del Fuoco (Fire Department)**
    - **Phone**: 115

It was comforting to know this number when I saw a local team managing a small brush fire outside the city. The efficiency and community spirit they showed were inspiring.

Pharmacies and After-Hours Care

If you need medication or minor medical assistance, pharmacies in Assisi are your best bet. One of the most helpful places I found was:

- **Farmacia Comunale Assisi**
    - **Address**: Via San Francesco, 18, 06081 Assisi PG, Italy
    - **Phone**: +39 075 812747

Many pharmacies in Italy display their operating hours on the door, along with details of the nearest pharmacy open after hours. I recall needing an antihistamine for an allergy flare-up and finding the process surprisingly easy. A local pharmacist even offered advice on nearby grocery stores for allergy-friendly food options—talk about going above and beyond!

For late-night emergencies, the **Guardia Medica** (after-hours medical service) is a lifesaver. You can contact them at **116117**. While I didn't personally need this service, a fellow traveler told me they received prompt and effective help when their child developed a sudden fever.

Transportation and Roadside Assistance

If you're exploring Assisi and its surroundings by car, having roadside assistance numbers can be invaluable. While my rental car experience went off without a hitch, I kept these numbers on hand:

- **ACI (Automobile Club d'Italia)**
    - **Phone**: 803116
    - This is Italy's version of AAA, providing breakdown services and assistance.

You'll also find local taxis helpful for late-night rides when buses stop running. One reliable service is:

- **Taxi Assisi**
    - **Phone**: +39 075 813100

The taxi drivers here are some of the friendliest I've encountered, and they always seem to have insider tips on hidden gems around town.

Tourist Assistance

Let's face it: sometimes, emergencies aren't life-threatening—they're just inconvenient. Like losing your wallet or needing urgent travel information. That's when a tourist information center can come to the rescue.

- **Tourist Information Office Assisi**
    - **Address**: Piazza del Comune, 22, 06081 Assisi PG, Italy
    - **Phone**: +39 075 812534

- o **Hours**: Usually open from 9 AM to 6 PM (confirm during holidays).

The staff here were incredibly helpful when I misplaced my guidebook. They offered me free maps, local recommendations, and even reassured me about finding my way to the bus stop.

Embassy Contacts

While Assisi doesn't have embassies within the city, Rome's embassies are your closest option for passport issues or legal matters. Keep these numbers handy if you're an international traveler.

For U.S. citizens:

- **U.S. Embassy in Rome**
  - o **Phone**: +39 06 46741

For U.K. citizens:

- **British Embassy in Rome**
  - o **Phone**: +39 06 4220001

For Australians:

- **Australian Embassy in Rome**
  - o **Phone**: +39 06 852721

Additional Tips

Before heading to Assisi, save these numbers on your phone and ensure you have an international roaming plan or access to Wi-Fi for calls. Many establishments in Assisi offer free Wi-Fi, so you won't be stranded if your mobile data fails.

Also, I highly recommend carrying a small phrasebook or downloading an app like Google Translate. While many locals speak English, showing an effort to speak Italian goes a long way in receiving warm assistance.

Printed in Dunstable, United Kingdom